New Mastermaths

Book 1

Paul Briten

OXFORD

OXFORD
UNIVERSITY PRESS

Great Clarendon Street, Oxford OX2 6DP

Oxford University Press is a department of the University of Oxford.
It furthers the University's objective of excellence in research, scholarship,
and education by publishing worldwide in

Oxford New York

Auckland Bangkok Buenos Aires Cape Town Chennai
Dar es Salaam Delhi Hong Kong Istanbul Karachi Kolkata
Kuala Lumpur Madrid Melbourne Mexico City Mumbai Nairobi
São Paulo Shanghai Taipei Tokyo Toronto

Oxford is a registered trade mark of Oxford University Press
in the UK and in certain other countries

New Mastermaths © Paul Briten 2004

British Library Cataloguing in Publication Data

Data available

ISBN 019 836111 4

10 9 8 7 6 5 4 3 2 1

Acknowledgments
Autumn Header Image © istockphoto (www.istockphoto.com)

Illustrated by IFA Design Ltd., Martin Chatterton
Cover design by Jonatronix
Page design by IFA Design Ltd., Plymouth UK
Printed in Italy by G. Canale & C.SpA

Contents

Introduction

The Mastermaths series will help you have fun practising all the maths you need to learn. Read this page first to see how to use the book.

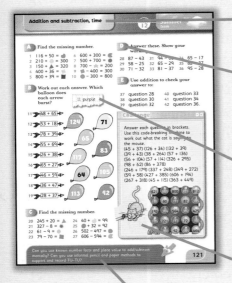

The title tells you what the page is about.

Work through the sections in order. Your teacher will tell you which questions to answer.

Some sections have examples to show how to set out your answer or remind you how to do the question. For sections with no example, you must choose your own method. Ask your teacher if you need help.

At the end of each page is a **Challenge**. Can you use the maths skills you have learned to solve the puzzles?

When you have finished working on a page, check that you can do this.

The **Think about it...** pages are fun games and activities for you to try.

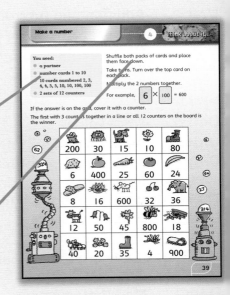

Check that you have everything you need before you start.

Read the instructions carefully to make sure you know what to do. Ask your teacher if you don't understand.

This book also contains six **Review** pages. Work through the questions in order to see if you have understood all the maths in the **Units**.

A Write in order, smallest first.

1 17 24 38 46 81

1	24	46	81	17	38
2	35	14	6	28	47
3	29	48	11	63	28
4	15	60	41	98	7
5	32	80	35	27	30
6	40	62	39	63	70

B Write in words.

7 twenty-seven

7	27	10	63		
8	81	11	72	13	18	15	11
9	40	12	96	14	49	

C Write in words the number on each sail.

16 four hundred and sixty-three

16 463 20 360 24 108
17 279 21 263 25 407
18 362 22 749 26 911
19 27 23 819

D Write in figures.

27 176

27 one hundred and seventy-six
28 four hundred and fifty-three
29 two hundred and seventy-seven
30 six hundred and sixteen
31 nine hundred and eighty-two
32 six hundred and sixty
33 three hundred and six

E Write how many hundreds, tens and units.

34 Three hundreds, five tens, eight units

34	358	37	685	40	834	42	380
35	364	38	432	41	407	43	500
36	519	39	917				

Challenge

Use number cards 1 to 9.
Turn over the top 3 cards. Write 6 different 2-digit numbers you can make with your 3 cards.
Write your 6 numbers in order, smallest first.
Shuffle the cards. Repeat 5 times.

6   3   8

For example, cards 6, 3 and 8 can make 36, 38, 63, 68, 83 and 86.

Can you read and write whole numbers to 1000 in figures and words?

A Write the next number.

1	267	4	307	7	599
2	328	5	685	8	909
3	411	6	639	9	246

`1  268`

B Write in digits.

`10  372`

10 3 hundreds 7 tens 2 units
11 2 hundreds 2 tens 3 units
12 7 hundreds 6 tens 9 units
13 4 hundreds 3 tens 8 units
14 1 hundred 0 tens 7 units
15 8 hundreds 4 tens 0 units

C Write the value of the blue digit.

16	659	20	973
17	327	21	976
18	542	22	640
19	368	23	839
		24	765

`16  fifty`

D Write who has more money.

25

Mr Rich £627 Mrs Cash £726

`25  Mrs Cash`

26

Bill £427 Jill £406

27

Ali £311 George £133

28

David £399 Jess £401

29

Asha £893 Ben £900

E Write how many children can each be given 10 sweets.

30 98 sweets
31 63 sweets
32 41 sweets   34 93 sweets
33 29 sweets   35 56 sweets

`30  9`

F Write how many packs of 100 nails can be made.

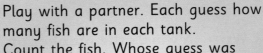

36 320 nails
37 240 nails
38 560 nails   40 540 nails
39 190 nails   41 880 nails

`36  3`

Challenge ⊟☒

Play with a partner. Each guess how many fish are in each tank.
Count the fish. Whose guess was closer for each tank?

Do you know what each digit represents in a 3-digit number?

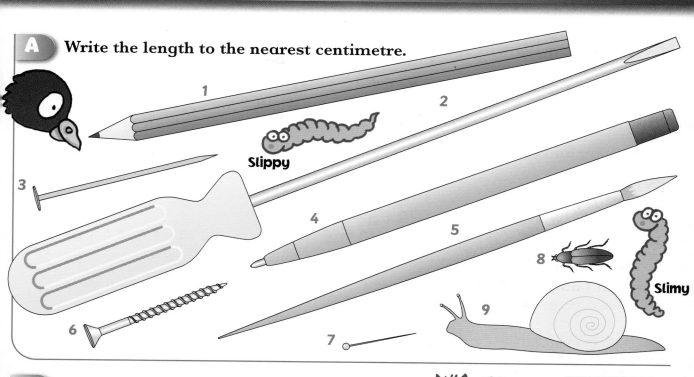

A Write the length to the nearest centimetre.

1

2

Slippy

3

4

5

8

Slimy

6

7

9

B Find roughly how much each object weighs.

10

12

14

10 2kg

Bendy

11

13

Challenge

Work with a partner. Use a ruler to measure in centimetres. Each guess the distance from the tip of the blackbird's beak to the red spot on Slippy's nose. Write down each guess. Measure the distance with the ruler. The closer guess scores a point. Repeat for the other 5 worms. The person with the most points is the winner.

Silk

C Write in words.

Glow

15	4695
16	3851
17	2760
18	4307
19	9048
20	3112
21	6007

15 four thousand
six hundred and
ninety-five

| 22 | 9413 | 24 | 1005 |
| 23 | 5672 | | |

Slider

A Answer these.

1 11

1 4 + 7	3 9 + 4	5 6 + 7	7 10 + 9	9 13 + 8
2 6 + 5	4 7 + 8	6 16 + 7	8 14 + 6	

B Copy and complete.

10 6 + 8 = 8 +
11 5 + 7 = 7 + ▲
12 8 + 4 = ✹ + 8
13 9 + 4 = 4 + ◖

14 6 + 7 = ● + 6
15 ● + 5 = 5 + 9
16 6 + 5 = ● + 6
17 8 + 10 = ◼ + 8

10 6 + 8 = 8 + 6

18 11 + 4 = 4 + ●

C Find how much money is in each bag.

19

21

20

22

E Write the total money in each purse.

29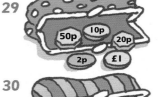

29 £1·82

30

32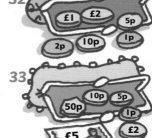

31

33

D Find how many coins you would get if you swapped:

23 5

23 the money in the red bag for £1 coins

24 the money in the blue bag for 50p coins

25 the money in the yellow bag for 20p coins

26 the money in the pink bag for £2 coins

27 the money in the blue bag for 1p coins

28 the money in the pink bag for 50p coins.

Challenge

Work out how to pay the exact amount for each item using 10 coins.

35p   48p   £12·20   £3·45

£1·15

Can you recognize all notes and coins and understand and use £.p notation?

A   Write how much money each has.

1   Asha   2   Jacob   3   Ella

B   Write how much money Asha would have if she was given another:

| 4 | £10·05 |

4   £1   6   £5
5   £2   7   50p   8   10p   9   20p

C   Write how much Jacob would have if he spent:

| 10 | £13·55 |

10   20p   12   £2
11   50p   13   £5   14   15p

D   If Ella gave Asha 50p:

15   write how much Ella would have
16   write how much Asha would have.

E   Find which children can pay exactly for:

| 17 | Asha and Jacob |

17   a game costing £1·55
18   a toy costing £2·70
19   a book costing £5·55
20   a comic costing 70p
21   a pen costing £2·60.

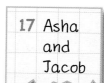

F   Solve these problems.

22   John has saved £26. He wants to buy a computer game costing £34. How much more money does he need?

23   Jess has £16. Her father gives her another £8. How much does she have now?

24   Henry has one note and one coin. His sister gives him a £1 coin. He now has £11·20. Which note and coin did Henry start with?

Challenge

Find out where this rocket will land. Follow the right answer.

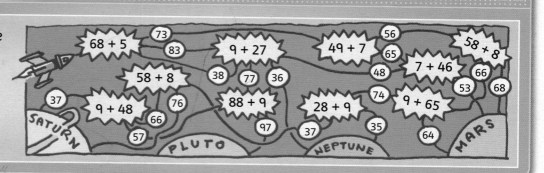

A Answer these.

[1 44]

1. 36 + 8 = ▲
2. 44 + 7 = ✿
3. 28 + 5 = ◗
4. 39 + 8 = ○
5. ○ = 6 + 28
6. 58 + ◆ = 65
7. ◖ = 72 + 4
8. ◻ + 36 = 42
9. ✳ = 8 + 29
10. ✳ + 67 = 74
11. 83 + ▲ = 91

B Find the answer.

[12 19]

12. subtract 3 from 22
13. subtract 6 from 57
14. what you must subtract from 92 to leave 87
15. 46 minus 9
16. count back 8 from 43
17. subtract 9 from 71
18. from 61 take away 6
19. subtract 7 from 90
20. how much less is 46 than 54

C Find the difference between:

[21 26]

21. 6 and 32
22. 4 and 51
23. 32 and 9
24. 7 and 43
25. 6 and 24
26. 61 and 5
27. 4 and 83
28. 62 and 7
29. 4 and 92
30. 85 and 6

D Answer these.

[31 34]

31. 41 − 7 = ◻
32. 36 − 9 = ●
33. 71 − ✳ = 65
34. ◻ = 51 − 8
35. ▲ = 62 − 9
36. 43 − ◖ = 37
37. ✿ = 28 − 9
38. 49 = 52 − ▲
39. 46 − ★ = 39

E Find how much money you will have.

[40 £34]

40. you have £18 and you are given £16
41. you have £25 and you are given £17
42. you have £33 and you spend £15
43. you have £46 and you spend £23
44. you have £16 and you are given £24
45. you have £29 and you are given £32

Challenge ▭ ⊠

Work out the sum on each arrow. Which colour balloon does not get burst?

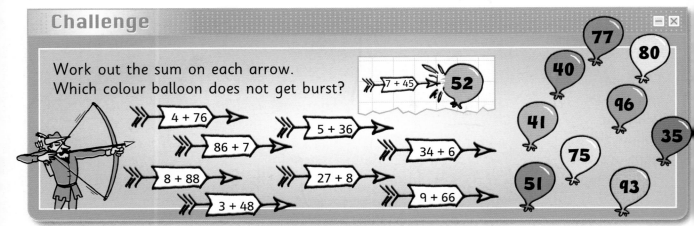

7 + 45 → 52

4 + 76 →
5 + 36 →
86 + 7 →
34 + 6 →
8 + 88 →
27 + 8 →
3 + 48 →
9 + 66 →

Balloons: 77, 80, 40, 96, 35, 41, 75, 51, 93

Can you read and begin to write related vocabulary for addition and subtraction?

A Write 3 coins that will pay exactly for:

1 57p

1 50p 5p 2p

2 £1·25

4 42p

3 90p

5 £2·15

B Write the fewest coins to pay exactly for:

6

6 £2 £1 20p

7 £1·83

10 £3·99

8 £1·98

11 £1·26

9 £4·87

12 £4·69

C Answer these.

13 11 + 12   18 15 + 16
14 6 + 7   19 45 + 46
15 14 + 15   20 24 + 26   23 36 + 35
16 20 + 21   21 15 + 13   24 29 + 30
17 25 + 26   22 42 + 44   25 32 + 33

13 23

D Solve these problems.

26 Ivor Fiver took £23 to the supermarket. After shopping he had £6 left. How much did he spend?

27 Concert tickets cost £9. What is the cost of 2 tickets?

28 Penny Pincher buys a comic for 85p. She gives a £1 coin to pay. How much change does she get?

29 Alex buys an ice-cream costing £1·50. How much change does he get from £5?

30 Jason has £8 more than Su. If Su has £15, how much money has Jason?

Challenge

Use these coins: one 50p, six 20p, two 10p, five 5p, four 2p and three 1p. Find how to pay the exact amount for each item.

82p   23p   85p

36p

Can you choose and use appropriate operations to solve word problems?

11

A   Write a number story for each.

> 1 Sarah saved £40. She spent £9 on a CD. She had £31 left.

1   40 − 9 = 31
2   30 − 7 = 23
3   23 − 9 = 14
4   18 + 7 = 25
5   33 + 8 = 41

6   62 − 7 = 55
7   20 − 12 = 8
8   17 + 9 = 26
9   14 + 13 = 27
10   26 + 27 = 53

B   Solve these problems.

11   Ali has 25p more than Bill. If Ali has 90p, how much has Bill?

12   On a school trip a teacher has £42. If she gives £1 pocket money to each of the 30 children, how much money will she have left?

13   Rob, Chloe and Jack are giving some money to a charity. Rob gives 48p, Chloe gives 46p and Jack gives £1. How much do they give altogether?

14   Beth has 24 books. If she gives away 7 of them, how many has she left?

C   Answer these.

15   Which is the cheapest item?
16   Which 4 coins could you use to pay the exact amount for the robot?
17   If you gave a £1 coin to pay for a set of teeth, how much change would you get?
18   Name 2 items that you could buy for £1.
19   Which 2 coins could you use to pay the exact amount for the skipping rope?
20   What is the total cost of a beard and a beetle?
21   What is the cost of a mask and a snake?
22   Which is cheaper, the mask or the beard?
23   Which is more expensive, the spider or the beetle?

Challenge

Amy's mum is buying Amy everything in the Fun Shop window except the skipping rope. Work out the fewest coins she can use when she pays.

Can you solve word problems and explain how the problem was solved?

A Find the total of each bill.

1

item	cost
onions	85p
lettuce	65p
carrots	75p

1 £2·25

2

item	cost
chicken	£2·50
juice	£1·10
apples	75p

3

item	cost
bread	82p
sausages	£1·45
butter	93p

B Find how many pence.

4 200

4 £2	7 £2·50
5 £5	8 £7·60
6 £6	9 £4·54

10 £5·12
11 £2·06

C Write in pounds.

12 472p	15 207p	18 605p
13 365p	16 382p	19 112p
14 912p	17 490p	20 379p

D Write coins that you could be given in change when:

21 1p 5p 20p

21 you spend £1·74 and give £2
22 you spend £2·83 and give £3
23 you spend £2·68 and give £5
24 you spend 68p and give £2
25 you spend £1·61 and give £5.

E Answer these.

26 Fred, Jenny and Sally want to buy a bunch of flowers costing £3·85. Fred has 95p, Jenny has £1·15 and Sally has 80p. How much more money will they need?

If a drink costs 48p, how much change would you get from:

27 £1   28 £2   29 £5?

Challenge

Play with a partner. Use number cards 0 to 9 and a large copy of this grid. Shuffle the cards. Take turns.
Place the top card in a space on the grid and leave it there.
Place the next two cards in the same way.
Write down the amount of money you have made.
The person with the larger amount scores a point.
Play 5 more games. The person with the most points is the champion.

£ ☐ . ☐ ☐

You need:
- a partner
- a dice
- a set of coins
- 2 sets of 4 counters

Each place a counter on the start square. Put the coins in the bank.

Take turns to roll the dice and count around the track.

When you land on a money square take a coin of that value.

When you can pay the exact money for an item in the shop, put the money in the bank and place a counter on the item.

The first to buy 3 items is the winner.

A Write each time.

1 quarter past ten

1

5

2

6

9

3

7

10

4

8

11

B Find out how long:

start time   **finish time**

12

Jason was walking

13

Carol was working

14

Lily was sleeping.

C Write what can take you about:

15   5 seconds   19   1 hour
16   30 seconds   20   2 hours
17   5 minutes   21   1 day.
18   $\frac{1}{2}$ hour

D Write the time that is:

22   1 hour earlier than 3 o'clock
23   1 hour later than 10:30
24   $\frac{1}{2}$ hour earlier than half past 3
25   $\frac{1}{2}$ hour later than quarter to 5
26   $\frac{1}{4}$ hour later than 3:30
27   $\frac{1}{4}$ hour earlier than quarter past 9.

E Write each time.

28 twenty past two

28

32

29

33

36

30

34

37

31

35

38

Challenge

How many minutes have passed since each clock showed 3 o'clock?

a   b   c   d   e   f

A To the nearest centimetre, guess the length each spider dropped.

1 Yoyo   2 Spooky   3 Webby   4 Creepy   5 Itzy   6 Jethr

B Measure to the nearest centimetre the length dropped by:

7 7 cm

7 Yoyo   8 Spooky   9 Webby   10 Creepy   11 Itzy   12 Jethro.

C Find the difference between your estimate and the measure for:

13 Creepy   15 Spooky   17 Itzy
14 Webby   16 Jethro   18 Yoyo.

D Draw a line this long:

19 $8\frac{1}{2}$ cm   21 6·5 cm   23 $11\frac{1}{2}$ cm
20 $4\frac{1}{2}$ cm   22 2·5 cm   24 7·5 cm.

E Solve these problems.

25 Shelley the snail crawls for 18 cm and then a further 22 cm. How far has Shelley crawled in total?

26 Two tables are placed end to end. The first table is 74 cm long and the second table is 82 cm long. What is the total length of the 2 tables?

27 A rope is 46 m long. If a length of 17 m is cut off, what length of rope is left?

28 What is the difference in length between a tow rope that is 8 m long and a tug of war rope that is 31 m long?

29 Bricks are 22 cm long. How far will 5 bricks stretch if they are placed end to end?

F Find how many centimetres.

30 1 m   31 2 m   32 4 m   33 $3\frac{1}{2}$ m   34 9 m   35 6·5 m   36 2·5 m

Challenge

a This robot is 1·5 m high and 90 cm wide. Could it walk forwards through your classroom door?

b This piece of string is 4·5 m long. Would it stretch across your classroom?

c This piece of fabric measures 1·5 m by 86 cm. Could it cover the top of your table?

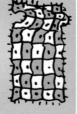

Can you choose an appropriate number operation and calculation method to solve word problems?

A Write each length in metres and centimetres.

1 1 m 36 cm

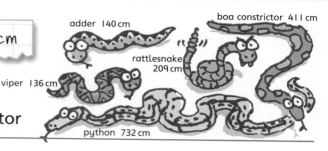

adder 140 cm

boa constrictor 411 cm

rattlesnake 209 cm

viper 136 cm

python 732 cm

1 the viper
2 the adder
3 the rattlesnake
4 the python
5 the boa constrictor

B Write in centimetres.

6 397 cm

6 3 m 97 cm
7 2 m 46 cm
8 6 m 42 cm
9 7 m 6 cm
10 4 m 8 cm
11 2·5 m
12 4 m 68 cm
13 8·5 m

C Solve these problems.

14 Raj is 1 m 43 cm tall and Jasmine is 186 cm tall. What is the difference in their heights?
15 A ladder is in 2 parts. The first part is 4·5 m long. The second part adds another 3 m 25 cm. What is the total height of the ladder?
16 Mo Torway is driving to see her friend who lives 55 km away. She has driven 9 km. How far has she still to travel?
17 In a 1 km race, Colin has run 400 m. How far has he left to run?

D 3 pieces of wood are placed end to end. Find the total length of these pieces:

18 80 cm, 1 m 10 cm and 45 cm
19 65 cm, 95 cm and 2 m
20 42 cm, 1 m 44 cm and 2·5 m
21 3·5 m, 2 m 25 cm and 65 cm
22 4·5 m, 3 m 28 cm and 72 cm.

E Find the difference in length between these snakes:

23 the adder and the python
24 the python and the boa
25 the rattlesnake and the python
26 the boa and the adder.

Challenge

Work with a partner. Use a metre rule. Measure each distance as accurately as you can in metres and centimetres:
• the length of your table
• the length of your classroom
• your height
• your partner's height
• the distance you walk in 5 paces
• the distance your partner walks in 5 paces.

A Name each 3D shape.

1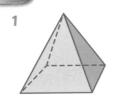

3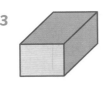

5

6

> 1 pyramid

2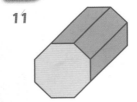

4

B Name the shape above which has:

7 2 flat circular faces and one curved face

8 8 vertices and 6 square faces

9 1 square face and 4 triangular faces

10 6 rectangular faces.

C Name each shape.

11

> 11 octagonal prism

12

13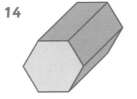

14

15

D Name a shape on this page that has:

> 16 pentagonal prism

16 2 pentagonal faces, 5 rectangular faces and 10 vertices

17 2 identical octagonal faces, 8 rectangular faces and 16 vertices

18 a circular face but is not a prism

19 6 square faces and 8 vertices

20 3 rectangular faces, 6 vertices and is a prism

21 has only a curved surface, no edges and no vertices

22 6 rectangular faces, 8 vertices and 12 edges.

Challenge — □ ✕

Name 3 different 3D shapes in each model.

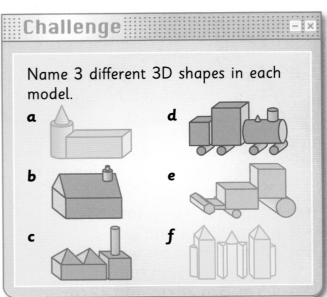

a

b

c

d

e

f

Can you classify and describe 3D shapes, referring to faces, edges and vertices?

A Name each 2D shape.

1

1 rectangle

2

5

3

6

4

7

B Write what colour shapes:

8 are quadrilaterals
9 contain 1 or more right angles.

C Part of each square is hidden.
Write the length of each side.

10

11

12

D Part of each rectangle is hidden.
Write the length of each side.

13

14

15

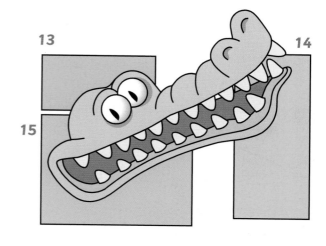

E Robo does not
understand what
a square is.

16 Describe a square
for Robo.

Challenge ▭ ⊠

On dotted paper draw:
a a square
b a hexagon
c an octagon
d a shape with
5 vertices
e a triangle that is
not a right-angled triangle
f a quadrilateral with 1 right angle
g a pentagon with 2 right angles
h a triangle with 2 sides the same
length.

A Find which colour line is the line of symmetry in each shape. Use a mirror.

1

3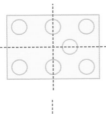

2

4

B Find how many dotted lines in each shape are lines of symmetry.

5

7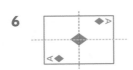

6

8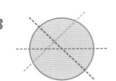

C Name the shape you can find if you imagine a mirror along each line of symmetry. Do not use a mirror.

9

11

10

12

D Use a mirror.

13 Check your answers to section C. Which questions did you get right?

E Find how many lines of symmetry are on each shape.

14

16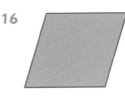

15

17

Challenge — □ ✕

a Write 10 capital letters that are symmetrical.
For example, D Y

b Write 3 letters that have 2 lines of symmetry.

c Use a mirror to work out this secret message:

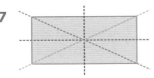

d Work out some more symmetrical words.

Can you classify and describe shapes referring to their reflective symmetry?

You need:
- a partner
- a set of number cards 1 to 9
- 2 sets of 8 counters

In turn, shuffle the cards and lay out the top 3 cards.

The number you make is the length of your fishing line in centimetres.

Choose a shape that you can reach with your line.

For example, if you make 486 cm, you can catch the triangle, square or hexagon.

If the name of your shape shows on the lighthouse, cover it with a counter.

The first to place 8 counters on the lighthouse is the winner.

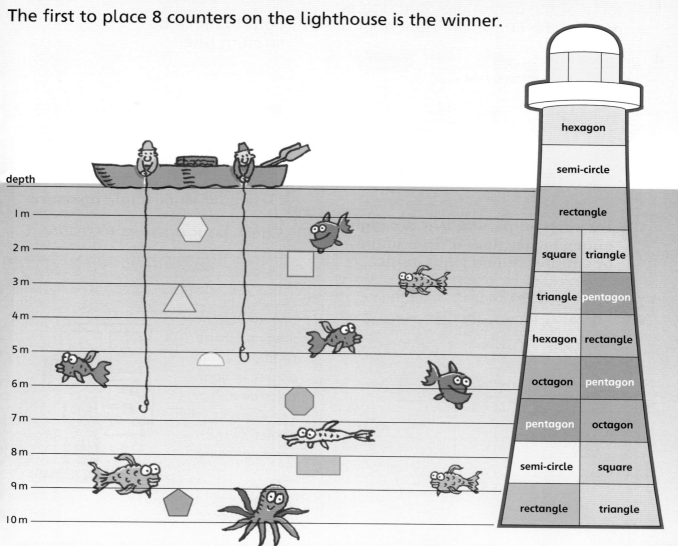

21

A Find how many angles in each shape are right angles.

 1 one

1  2   3 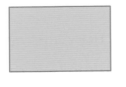 4 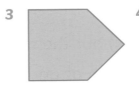 5

B Write the colours of these shapes in which:

6 all of the angles are right angles
7 some of the angles are right angles
8 none of the angles are right angles.

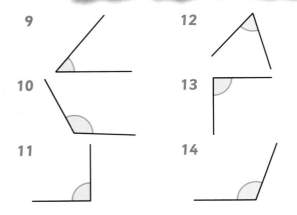

C For each angle, say if it is a right angle, larger than a right angle or smaller than a right angle.

9 smaller than a right angle

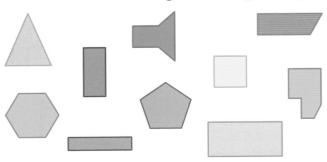

9   12
10   13
11   14

D Use a piece of paper to make a right-angle measure.

15 Fold to make a straight line.

16 Fold along the edge to make a right-angle.

E Use your right-angle measure.

17 Check your answers to section C.

Challenge ▭ ✕

Use your right-angle measure to find 20 right angles in your classroom.
For example, the corner of the window frame.

Can you identify right angles in 2D shapes and in the environment?

A Write how each person must move, so that they are not eaten by a monster!

1 1 square left, 1 square down, 2 squares left, 1 square up, 1 square left

1 Guide Tom to the coin.
2 Guide Bill to the gold.
3 Guide Ali to the coin.
4 Guide Jane to the diamond.
5 Guide Kate to the treasure.

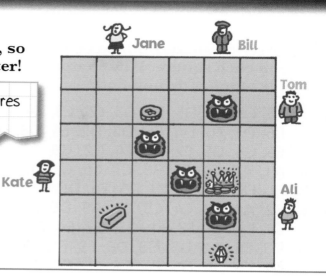

B Find which coin is in each square.

6 20p

6	E3	9	F4	12	AI	15	F6
7	A2	10	C5	13	B2	16	E5
8	E6	11	D3	14	C4	17	B3

C Name the square each place is in.

18 B4

18 the church
19 the hospital
20 the sports centre
21 the supermarket
22 the swimming pool
23 the school
24 the football ground

25 the library
26 Which squares does Town Road pass through?

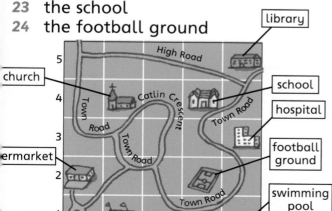

Challenge

a Copy this grid onto cm-squared paper.
b Write each letter of the alphabet in a different square on your grid.
c Write the position of each letter. For example, A is on square C6.

Can you describe and find the position of a square on a grid of squares with the rows and columns labelled?

23

A Use 16 counters. Place one on each square. What letter or number do you find?

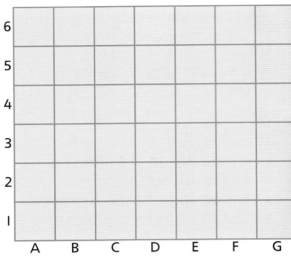

1 E6, C6, C2, D5, E2, D3, C5, C3, C4
2 B6, D1, F6, D4, C6, D5, D2, E6, D3, D6
3 E6, G4, G5, F2, G3, F4, G2, G6, E2, F6
4 A1, A5, C4, E5, B5, C1, C5, C2, D5, C3, B1
5 F1, E6, F2, D4, F3, D5, F4, D6, F5, E4, F6
6 B2, A2, B3, C4, C5, C2, A5, D5, D2, B5
7 E3, E1, G1, F3, F1, G3, G2, E4, E5, F5, G5
8 D3, E3, D4, D5, G3, D6, F3, F1, F4, F2
9 C4, E6, D4, D6, E4, C6, C5, C3, C2, D2, E2
10 B5, B4, B3, B2, B1, E1, E5, E2, E3, E4

B Look at the diagram below.

11 Imagine each square on this diagram is a locker. Each child in your class needs a locker. Write the names of the children in your class. By each name write the position of their locker.

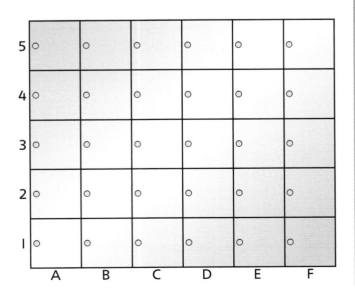

Can you read and begin to write the vocabulary of position?

Review 1

A   Write in words.

1 **246**   3 **409**   5 **411**   7 **806**

2 **328**   4 **320**   6 **560**

B   Write in figures.

8   two hundred and fifty-three
9   six hundred and nineteen
10   eight hundred and seven

C   Write the value of the red digit.

11   632   13   361   15   976
12   849   14   255   16   542

D   Write the amount of money in each purse.

17    18

E   Answer these.

19   64 + 7 = ●   24   33 − 7 = ▲
20   36 + 8 = ●   25   ■ = 61 − 8
21   ● + 9 = 43   26   36 − ■ = 28
22   65 + ■ = 74   27   73 = 81 − ★
23   ● = 83 + 7

F   Write four coins that will make each amount.

28   82p   30   95p   32   £3·30
29   £1·16   31   £2·07   33   £1·71

G   Answer these.

34   26 + 25   36   46 + 45   38   35 + 37
35   42 + 43   37   29 + 31

H   Write a number story for each.

39   54 − 8 = 46   41   41 − 8 = 33
40   25 + 27 = 52

I   Write in pounds.

42   283p   44   630p   46   413p
43   198p   45   809p   47   372p

J   Write each time.

48   49   50

K   Draw each line.

51   $6\frac{1}{2}$ cm long   53   10·5 cm long
52   8·5 cm long

L   Write in centimetres.

54   3 m 26 cm   56   5·5 m
55   4 m 16 cm   57   2 m 9 cm

M   Name each 2D shape.

58   59   60

N   Answer this.

61   Write two things that are true for all squares.

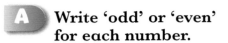
A Write 'odd' or 'even' for each number.

1 odd

1	27	4	62	7	26
2	38	5	11	8	33
3	43	6	9	9	55

B Write the next 3 numbers in each sequence.

10 20, 22, 24

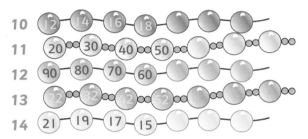

10 (12) (14) (16) (18)
11 (20) (30) (40) (50)
12 (90) (80) (70) (60)
13 (22) (32) (2) (2)
14 (21) (19) (17) (15)

C Write the missing number in each sequence.

15 4, 8 ▨, 16, 20   18 6, 8, 10, ▨, 14
16 6, 9, ▨, 15, 18   19 20, ●, 40, 50, 60
17 10, 15, ▨, 25, 30

D Find how many pencils in each group.

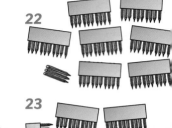

20

21

22

23

E Find how many:

24 wheels

25 wheels

26 legs

27 legs

28 toes.

Challenge   – x

Play with a partner. Use 2 dice and 2 counters.
Choose who is 'odd' and who is 'even'.
Place your counters in the start squares.
Take turns. Roll the 2 dice. Add the numbers together.
For example, ⚄ ⚂ , 5 + 3 = 8
If the number is even, the 'even' player moves one place towards the treasure.
If it is odd, the 'odd' player moves.
Who reaches the treasure first?

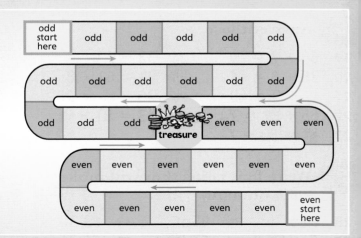

odd start here	odd	odd	odd	odd	odd
odd	odd	odd	odd	odd	odd
odd	odd	odd	treasure	even	even	even
even	even	even	even	even	even
even	even	even	even	even	even start here

A Find the number you reach when you count on:

1 9 from 64
2 10 from 85
3 12 from 61

1 73

4 15 from 105
5 7 from 96
6 20 from 47
7 13 from 108.

B Write the next 3 numbers in each sequence.

8 87 97 107

8 47, 57, 67, 77, ★, ★, ★,
9 63, 73, 83, 93, ●, ●, ●,
10 120, 130, 140, 150, ●, ●, ●,
11 48, 58, 68, 78, ▲, ▲, ▲,
12 94, 84, 74, 64, ■, ■, ■,
13 142, 132, 122, 112, ⬡, ⬡, ⬡,

C Write the number that is:

14 10 more than 50
15 10 more than 32
16 10 more than 96

14 60

17 10 less than 54
18 10 less than 93
19 10 less than 108.

D Write the number that is:

20 8 tens
21 7 tens
22 10 tens
23 12 tens
24 14 tens
25 20 tens

20 80

26 15 tens.

E Write the next 3 numbers in each sequence.

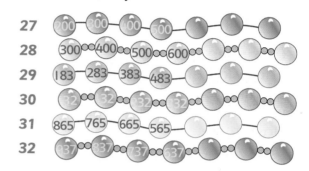

27 200 300 400 500
28 300 400 500 600
29 183 283 383 483
30 32 32 32 32
31 865 765 665 565
32 837 837 737 637

F Find how much is left.

33 £750

33 Jackie has £850 and spends £100.
34 Jem has £224 and spends £10.
35 Manzil has £526 and spends £100.
36 Jason has £720 and spends £300.
37 Ethel has £103 and spends £20.
38 Anish has £735 and spends £400.

Challenge

Write in order the missing numbers. In the yellow circles find the letter by each answer. Write the correct letter under each answer to find a hidden question. Answer the question.

a 64, 74, 84, ✳, 104, ✳, ✳
b 121, 221, ●, ●, 521, 621, 721
c ▲, ▲, 124, 114, 104, 94, ▲
d 821, 721, ⬡, ⬡, 421, 321, ⬡
e 64, ●, 44, 34, 24, 14, ●

54 E   421 U   321 O   144 H   134 A   4 T
94 D   114 O   621 E   521 A   124 Y   221 P   84 V

A Toto is visiting from Argon. Describe for Toto:

1 an odd number
2 an even number.

B Toto cannot speak. He has sent you a code to say he can understand odd numbers.

3 Cover the odd numbers on his code with counters. Has he understood?

248	38	64	126	520
362	510	488	324	869
116	28	360	483	512
69	200	327	14	450
778	111	636	412	826

C Find what odd numbers you can get when you:

4   3, 5, 7, 9, 11

4 roll 2 dice and add the numbers
5 roll 3 dice and add the numbers
6 roll 4 dice and add the numbers.

D Write these numbers.

7 2 different numbers you can add together to make 16
8 3 different odd numbers you can add together to make 19
9 3 different even numbers you can add together to make 30
10 4 odd numbers you can add together to make 100

E Answer these. Explain how you know.

11 Would 28 be in this sequence?

4 — 8 — 12 — 16 —

12 Would 65 be in this sequence?
15 °° 20 °° 25 °° 30 °°

13 Would 70 be in this sequence?
7 — 17 — 27 — 37 —

14 Would 21 be in this sequence?
22 °° 22 °° 22 °° 22 °°

Challenge ▭ ☒

Play with a partner. Use number cards 1 to 9 and a dice.
Take turns. Turn over the top card. This is the first number in your sequence.
Roll the dice. This number tells you the steps to take in your sequence.
Score a point if the number 10, 15 or 20 is in your sequence.
The first to score 10 points is the winner.
For example,

6
6 10 14 18 22
↑ score 1 point

4
4 6 8 10 12 14 16 18 20
↑ score 2 points ↑

Can you solve number puzzles?

A Double the number on each shirt.

1  9

4  12

2  11

5 16

3 15

6  20

C Write a multiplication to answer these.

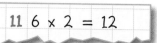
11 6 × 2 = 12

11 Find how many ears.

12 Find how many legs.

13 Find how many legs.

B Only half of each group of flies is caught in the web. Find how many are caught.

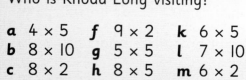

7

8

9

10

D Write 2 multiplication facts for each array.

14 3 × 4 = 12   4 × 3 = 12

14

15

16

17

Challenge

Use a set of 14 counters.
Answer each question.
Cover each answer with
a counter.
Who is Rhoda Long visiting?

a 4 × 5 **f** 9 × 2 **k** 6 × 5
b 8 × 10 **g** 5 × 5 **l** 7 × 10
c 8 × 2 **h** 8 × 5 **m** 6 × 2
d 6 × 10 **i** 7 × 2 **n** 9 × 5
e 7 × 5 **j** 5 × 10

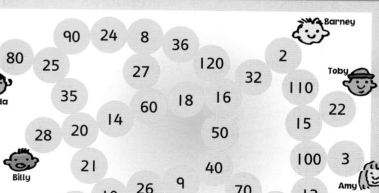

Can you understand multiplication as repeated addition and as an array?

29

Multiplication and division

A Copy and complete each sequence.

1	9	12	15	18
	21	24	27	30

1 9, 12, ⭐, 18, 21 ⭐, ⭐, 30
2 3, 6, 9, ⬡, ⬡, ⬡, 21, 24
3 15, ▲, 21, 24, ▲, ▲, 33, 36
4 0, 🍎, 🍎, 9, 12, 15, 18, 🍎

B Answer these.

5	15

5 3 × 5 = ⭐
6 3 × 3 = ✳
7 3 × 7 = ●
8 3 × 9 = ▪
9 3 × 10 = ▲
10 3 × ✳ = 12
11 3 × ⬡ = 18

C Find the total number of legs.

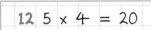 12 5 × 4 = 20

12 5 giraffes
13 6 lions
14 8 tigers
15 3 cats
16 7 dogs
17 10 horses
18 4 elephants
19 9 zebra

D Copy and complete.

20 3 × 10 = 10 × 3

20 3 × 10 = 10 × ✳
21 4 × 5 = ⭐ × 4
22 3 × 5 = 5 × ⬡
23 5 × 10 = ▪ × 5
24 ▲ × 5 = 5 × 7
25 6 × ● = 4 × 6
26 10 × ⬟ = 2 × 10
27 3 × 4 = ✳ × 3

E Find how many.

28 7 times 5
29 2 multiplied by 7
30 8 lots of 10
31 the product of 5 and 8
32 9 groups of 3
33 double 12
34 4 × 8
35 5 multiplied by 9
36 6 times 4

Challenge

Each quarter of this target has a number: 3, 4, 5 or 10.
In a paint splatting contest the yellow ring scores a single, the pink ring scores double and the green ring scores treble (× 3).
For example, red splats scored 3 + 20 + 12 = 35.
Find how many points were scored by:

a blue splats
b black splats
c green splats
d brown splats.

Work out how three splats could score:

e 21
f 44
g 27
h 32.

Do you understand that multiplication can be done in any order?

A Solve these problems.

1 A worm is 3 times longer than a spider. If the spider is 3 cm long, how long is the worm?

2 Jackie has 10p. Billy has 4 times as much. How much money does Billy have?

3 Alex works for 2 hours and his dad works 5 times as long. For how many hours does his dad work?

4 A red parcel weighs 4 kg. A green parcel weighs 10 times as much. How much does the green parcel weigh?

B Answer these.

5 $4 \times 10 = $ ✳
6 $6 \times 10 = $ ▲
7 $9 \times 10 = $ ⬡
8 $7 \times $ ⬣ $ = 70$
9 $10 \times 10 = $ 🌰

10 $11 \times 10 = $ ▲
11 ▪ $ \times 10 = 130$
12 $15 \times 10 = $ ★

`5  40`

C Find how many pennies have the same value.

`13  300`

13

14

15

16

D Answer these.

`17  1400`

17 $14 \times 100 = $ ★
18 $12 \times 100 = $ ▪
19 $15 \times 100 = $ ✳
20 $19 \times $ ⬣ $ = 1900$
21 $700 \div 100 = $ ☁
22 $300 \div 100 = $ ⬡
23 $800 \div $ ▲ $ = 8$
24 $200 \div 10 = $ ★
25 $200 \div 100 = $ ✳

Challenge

Use 30 counters.

Cover the multiples of 10 on the yellow grid.

Cover the multiples of 100 on the green grid.

Cover the multiples of 5 on the pink grid.

What creature do you find?

50	80	100	600	800	200	25	4	63
30	22	34	300	250	120	5	26	92
70	90	40	400	700	300	50	32	18
20	56	78	900	550	640	15	48	64
60	40	10	500	100	300	35	30	45

You need:

- a partner
- 2 sets of 10 counters
- a set of 6 cards with the letters A–F
- a set of 6 number cards 1–6

Shuffle both sets of cards and lay them face down.
Each choose a playing card at the bottom of the page.
Turn over the top card in each pile. This is the position of a
question on the grid.
For example, C5 is question $3 \times 9 = $ ★.
If the answer is on your card or your partner's card, cover it with a counter.
The first to have 10 counters on their card is the winner.

	A	B	C	D	E	F
6	$63 + 8 = $ ⬤	$6 \times 100 = $ ⬡	$4 \times 4 = $ ▲	$9 \times 5 = $ ◼	$36 - 9 = $ ✳	$4 \times 10 = $ ⬤
5	$3 \times 8 = $ ★	$6 \times 5 = $ ✳	$3 \times 9 = $ ★	$4 \times 9 = $ ▲	✳ $+ 6 = 33$	$24 + 25 = $ ★
4	▲ $+ 6 = 41$	$4 \times 7 = $ ⬤	$42 - 5 = $ ⬡	$65 = 72 - $ ◼	$10 \times 8 = $ ⬤	$106 - 10 = $ ◼
3	$25 + 27 = $ ✳	$6 \times $ ⬤ $= 60$	$43 + 10 = $ ✳	$3 \times 6 = $ ▲	★ $= 63 + 8$	$8 \times $ ✳ $= 40$
2	$7 \times 5 = $ ▲	$37 - $ ✳ $= 29$	$10 \times 10 = $ ★	$45 + 46 = $ ⬡	$8 \times 4 = $ ◼	⬤ $- 10 = 72$
1	$83 + 10 = $ ▲	$5 \times 5 = $ ★	$56 - $ ✳ $= 47$	$5 \times 7 = $ ▲	⬤ $\times 5 = 20$	$9 \times 100 = $ ◼

A			
93	35	25	4
27	8	10	52
71	82	900	49

C			
32	37	8	80
9	27	28	53
35	16	100	91

E			
5	30	71	40
24	45	27	600
7	35	36	96

A   Copy and complete.

1

×	3	2
4		
5		

3

×	10	100
6		
4		

2

×	3	10	2
5			
10			
4			

4

×	3	4	100
3			
4			
5			

B   Find the cost.

5   £9

5   3 cars
6   4 puppets
7   9 bats and balls
8   10 comics
9   8 CDs
10 100 cars
11 12 CDs

£3
£4
£5
£1
£10

C   Find the total cost.

12   £13

12   3 cars and 4 comics
13   2 puppets and 3 cars
14   4 bats and balls and 6 CDs
15   6 puppets and 4 cars
16   3 bats and balls and 7 puppets

D   You have £20. How many can you buy?

17   comics
18   CDs
19   puppets
20   bats and balls

17   20

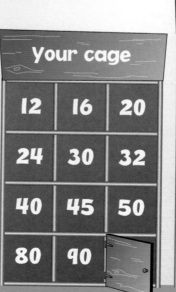

Your cage

12	16	20
24	30	32
40	45	50
80	90	

Monster's cage

14	18
21	27
28	35
36	60
70	100

Do you know by heart the multiplication facts for the 2, 3, 4, 5 and 10 times tables?

33

A Solve these problems. Show your working.

1 Louise saves 10p every day towards a CD player. How much does she save in 8 days?

2 If Rosie Peel buys 4 apples for 20p each, how much does she spend?

3 How many horseshoes do you need for 7 horses?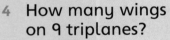

4 How many wings on 9 triplanes?

5 I think of a number and multiply it by 8. My answer is 32. What is my number?

6 How many legs are there on 10 spiders?

7 How many legs on 100 spiders?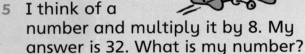

8 Glasses cost £3 each. How many can you buy for £20?

9 Oliver saves 50p a week towards a football. If a football costs £12, for how many weeks will Oliver have to save?

10 If you have £20, do you have enough money to buy 6 melons at £3 each?

11 On a ride there are 10 people in each car. How many people are there in 15 cars?

12 Theatre tickets cost £30. What is the cost of 4 tickets?

13 Omar has £30. He gives £12 to his sister. How much has he left?

14 There are 50 seeds in a packet. How many seeds are in 6 packets?

15 A lorry can carry 300 paving stones. How many paving stones can the lorry carry in 3 trips?

Challenge ☐☒

Find 3 numbers from this set to make a number sentence.
For example, 6 × 4 = 24.
How many different number sentences can you make?

6	5	10	4	8
3	14	24	40	16

Can you choose the appropriate number operation and calculation method to solve word problems?

A
Write a story question to match each number sentence.

> 1 Hexagons have six sides. How many sides are there on 3 hexagons?

1 $3 \times 6 = 18$
2 $4 \times 7 = 28$
3 $9 \times 3 = 27$
4 $10 \times 9 = 90$
5 $4 \times 100 = 400$

6 $5 \times 8 = 40$
7 $20 \div 5 = 4$
8 $100 \div 10 = 10$
9 $24 \div 6 = 4$

B
Answer these. Then multiply in a different order to check.

> 10 30 $3 \times 10 = 30$

10 10×3
11 4×5
12 5×10

13 4×3
14 10×4

15 100×5
16 2×6

C
Solve these problems. Show your working.

17 A class of children are split into teams of 4. How many children will there be in 7 teams?

18 I think of a number, find half of it and subtract 16. My answer is 6. What is my number?

19 Tilly Vision watches 4 films, each lasting 30 minutes. For how many minutes does she watch the films?

20 If boxes can hold 8 pears, how many boxes will be needed for 48 pears?

21 Joe has £15. He buys 3 drinks costing 40p each. How much money has he left?

22 If there are 40 drawing pins in a box, how many drawing pins are there in 10 boxes?

Challenge

Work out the numbers missing on each target.

a 8 9 2 4 6 7 4 5 3 8 12

b 50 40 9 70 4 10 8 30 6 20

c 18 24 3 10 6 6 54 7 30 48

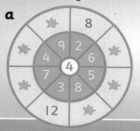
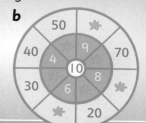
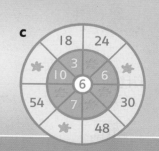

Can you check your answers to multiplication problems by multiplying in a different order?

35

A Find what fraction is yellow.

  $1\frac{1}{2}$

1

5

2

6

3

7

4

B Find which coloured shape has been divided into:

8 the green shape

8 quarters

9 thirds

10 halves

11 fifths

12 tenths.

C Find how many marbles in:

13 6

13 $\frac{1}{2}$ of this group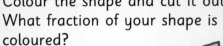

14 $\frac{1}{2}$ of this group

15 $\frac{1}{4}$ of this group

16 $\frac{1}{3}$ of this group

17 $\frac{1}{5}$ of this group

18 $\frac{1}{10}$ of this group.

Challenge

Use paper and scissors.
a   Fold a piece of paper in half. Draw a shape against the fold. Colour the shape and cut it out. What fraction of your shape is coloured?
b   Fold a piece of paper in half and half again. Draw a shape against the corner. Colour the shape and cut it out. What fraction of your shape is coloured?
c   Make an interesting bookmark.

Can you recognize the fractions $\frac{1}{2}$, $\frac{1}{3}$, $\frac{1}{4}$, $\frac{1}{5}$, $\frac{1}{10}$, and use them to find fractions of shapes and numbers?

A Find how many pizzas will give:

1 8 halves
2 8 quarters
3 12 thirds
4 10 fifths
5 20 tenths
6 20 quarters.

B Find what fraction of each shape is red.

7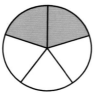

8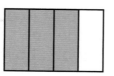

9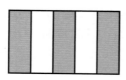

10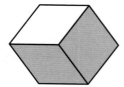

11

12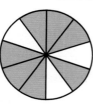

C Write in figures.

 $13\frac{3}{5}$

13 three fifths
14 three quarters
15 two fifths
16 three tenths
17 two thirds
18 seven tenths
19 four fifths

D Copy onto squared paper. Colour the fraction shown.

20 $\frac{1}{3}$

21 $\frac{3}{4}$

22 $\frac{3}{5}$

23  $\frac{7}{10}$

Challenge

Copy these shapes onto squared paper. Colour them as asked.
How many small squares are not coloured on each shape?

a Colour $\frac{1}{2}$ red, $\frac{1}{10}$ blue, $\frac{1}{4}$ yellow.

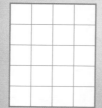

b Colour $\frac{2}{5}$ yellow, $\frac{1}{4}$ green, $\frac{3}{10}$ blue.

Can you begin to recognize fractions that are several parts of a whole?

$1\frac{1}{3}$

A Write a fraction to show how much each person gets when a cake is divided equally:

1 among 3 people
2 among 5 people
3 among 4 people
4 among 10 people
5 between 2 people.

B Solve these problems.

6 There are 20 children in the chess club. Three quarters of the children are boys. How many boys are in the club?

7 There are 12 birds in a garden. If $\frac{2}{3}$ of them are sparrows, how many sparrows are there?

8 Mrs Munch eats three tenths of a box of chocolates. If there were 30 chocolates in the box, how many does she eat?

9 Paulo eats $\frac{3}{5}$ of a pizza. What fraction of the pizza is left?

10 In a class of 30 children, $\frac{2}{5}$ are girls. How many boys are in the class?

11 Bill has £24. He spends one quarter of his money on a cap. How much money has he left?

12 Honor Trek is taking part in a 10-mile walk. After she has completed $\frac{3}{5}$ of the walk, how far has she still to walk?

13 Out of 100 football fans, $\frac{7}{10}$ wear red scarves. The rest wear blue scarves. How many fans wear blue scarves?

Challenge

Follow the correct answers to find out where the plane is landing.

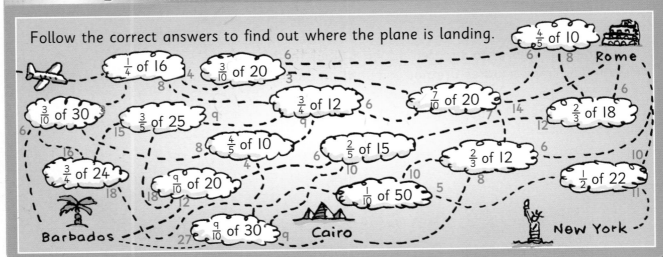

Can you use fractions that are several parts of a whole?

You need:

- a partner
- number cards 1 to 10
- 10 cards numbered 2, 3, 4, 4, 5, 5, 10, 10, 100, 100
- 2 sets of 12 counters

Shuffle both packs of cards and place them face down.

Take turns. Turn over the top card on each pack.

Multiply the 2 numbers together.

For example, $6 \times 100 = 600$

If the answer is on the grid, cover it with a counter.

The first with 3 counters together in a line or all 12 counters on the board is the winner.

200	30	15	10	80
6	400	25	60	24
8	16	600	32	36
12	50	45	800	18
40	20	35	4	900

A Find the missing number.

1 14

1 $6 + \star = 20$
2 $11 + \blacksquare = 20$
3 $70 + 20 = \star$
4 $40 + \blacksquare = 100$ 8 $8 + 6 + \blacksquare = 20$
5 $5 + 14 = \bullet$ 9 $2 + \bullet + 7 = 18$
6 $36 + 10 = \bullet$ 10 $8 - 6 = \triangle$
7 $5 + 3 + 6 = \bullet$ 11 $9 - 4 = \bullet$
  12 $8 - \pentagon = 2$

B Write 2 addition facts and 2 subtraction facts for each.

13 $7 + 6 = 13$
14 $9 + 7 = 16$
15 $5 + 8 = 13$
16 $12 + 6 = 18$
17 $21 + 12 = 33$
18 $7 + 19 = 26$

13 $7 + 6 = 13$
$6 + 7 = 13$
$13 - 6 = 7$
$13 - 7 = 6$

C Work out the difference between the 2 numbers on each plane.

19 8

19   204   196

20   502   499

23   202   199

21   603   597

24   805   797

25   906   894

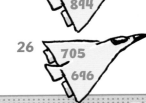
22   701   698

26   705   696

Challenge

Use a set of counters and a large copy of this grid. Answer each question. Cover the answers in the grid with counters to find out who robbed the bank.

1	7	13	19	25	31	37	43	49	55	75
2	8	14	20	26	32	38	44	50	56	80
3	9	15	21	27	33	39	45	51	57	85
4	10	16	22	28	34	40	46	52	60	90
5	11	17	23	29	35	41	47	53	65	95
6	12	18	24	30	36	42	48	54	70	100

Rod   **Bud**   **Jed**   **Sid**

Rod	Bud	Jed			
$60 + 20$	$43 + 10$	$31 - 3$	$65 + 20$	$502 - 498$	$4 + 5 + 8$
$39 + 3$	$100 - 5$	$31 + 21$	$13 - 8$	$80 - 40$	$20 - 4$
$8 - 5$	$50 - 20$	$90 - 30$	$20 - 10$	$5 + 13$	$18 - 12$
$40 + 50$	$20 + 16$	$35 + 19$	$201 - 199$	$22 + 19$	$34 + 36$
$60 + 40$	$19 + 10$	$80 - 5$	$60 - 59$	$16 - 4$	

 Do you understand that subtraction is the inverse of addition?

A Guess how long it would take you to:

1 walk to the playground and back
2 count to 20
3 read 5 pages of your reading book
4 grow an inch

5 eat your lunch
6 write your full name
7 walk a mile.

B Solve these problems.

8 Alan starts gardening at half past one. He finishes at quarter to four. For how long is he gardening?
9 Laura starts swimming at 10:10. She finishes at 11:00. For how long is she swimming?

10 Jane's bus journey takes 25 minutes. If she arrives at ten past six, at what time does she leave?
11 Carrie Jezz needs to be at the station at 10:15. If it takes her 35 minutes to walk to the station, at what time should she leave?
12 Playtime lasts for 15 minutes. If it ends at 11:05, at what time does it start?

Challenge

Follow each correct arrow. Write the letters in order. Discover the secret message. For example, 1 year = 365 days, so write the letter D.

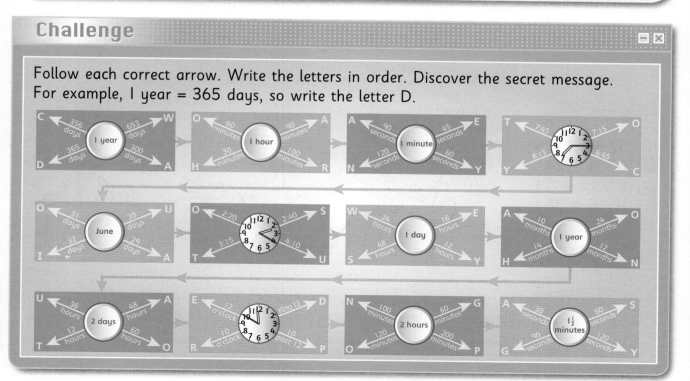

Can you use units of time and the relationship between them?

The Beach Shop

£10

£7·50

CONCERT TONIGHT 7.00

£30

£2·50

A Answer these questions. Show your working.

1 Emil has £25. He buys a beach ball. How much has he left?
2 Vicky buys a concert ticket with a £10 note. How much change will she get?
3 A rope is 27 m long. If 18 m is cut off, what length of rope is left?

4 Ants have 6 legs. How many legs are there on 5 ants?

B Check each answer with an addition.

> 5 $11 + 7 = 18$

5 $18 - 7 = 11$
6 $21 - 6 = 15$
7 $80 - 30 = 50$
8 $34 - 11 = 23$

9 $45 - 6 = 39$
10 $19 - 7 = 12$

C Make up a number story to match each number sentence.

> 11 Ali collected 16 minibeasts. She gave 7 to Shelley and had 9 left.

11 $16 - 7 = 9$
12 $32 + 19 = 51$
13 $6 \times 4 = 24$
14 $4 \times 12 = 48$
15 $6 \times 6 = 36$

D Solve these problems.

16 There are 28 children in a class. Half of them are boys. If half the boys go to Games, how many children are left in the class?
17 Ashley has £140. He visits the Beach Shop and buys 2 beach balls and 2 pairs of beach shoes. How much has he left?
18 Ella wants to buy 2 concert tickets and a surf-board. She has £44. Does she have enough money?

Challenge ▬ ☒

Each person spends some money at the Beach Shop. Jody spends £17·50. Arthur spends £20. Eleanor spends £35. Sasha spends £22·50. Ben spends £57·50. Work out what each person could buy. For example, Jody could buy a ball and 3 pairs of beach shoes.

Can you choose appropriate number operations and calculation methods to solve word problems?

A Find how many children in Year 3 have joined:

1 the art club
2 the chess club
3 the football club
4 the drama club
5 the netball club
6 Find the total number of children who have joined a club.
7 Find how many more children joined the chess club than the drama club.

`1 2`

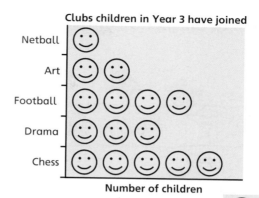

Clubs children in Year 3 have joined

Netball
Art
Football
Drama
Chess

Number of children

☺ = 1 person

8 Name the most popular club.

B Answer these.

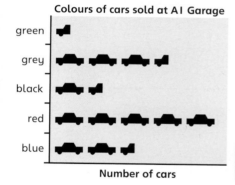

Colours of cars sold at A1 Garage

green
grey
black
red
blue

Number of cars

🚗 = 2 cars
🚗 = 1 car

9 How many green cars were sold?
10 How many red cars were sold?
11 How many cars were sold altogether?
12 How many more grey cars than blue cars were sold?
13 How many fewer black cars than red cars were sold?
14 How many of the cars sold were either grey or black?
15 Which was the most popular colour?

Challenge

Use the frequency table. Copy and complete the pictogram.

Coins in Jenny Jingle's purse	Frequency
1p	3
2p	4
5p	7
10p	5
20p	2
50p	4
£1	6
£2	2

● = 2 coins
❘ = 1 coin

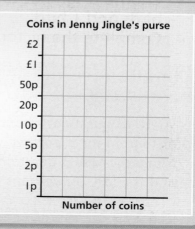

Coins in Jenny Jingle's purse

£2
£1
50p
20p
10p
5p
2p
1p

Number of coins

Can you interpret data in frequency tables and in pictograms with the symbol representing 2 units?

43

A **Look at the picture of the birds.**

1 Copy and complete this frequency table to show how many of each bird.

Bird	Frequency
duck	
woodpecker	
gull	
swan	
robin	
heron	

B **Look at this pictogram.**

2 Copy the pictogram.
3 Choose a symbol to stand for 2 birds and 1 bird.
4 Complete the pictogram.

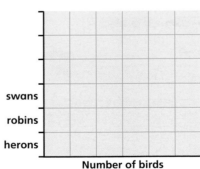

swans

robins

herons

Number of birds

= 2 birds

= 1 bird

Challenge ⊟☒

Write 10 questions about your pictogram for a partner.
Make the first 3 questions easy and the last 3 questions difficult!

Can you solve a problem by organizing and interpreting data in frequency tables and in pictograms with the symbol representing 2 units?

A Look at the spooky scene.

1 Copy and complete this frequency table to show how many of each creature.

Creature	Frequency
ant	
spider	
worm	
fly	
bird	
mouse	

B Use your frequency table.

2 Write 5 questions for a partner.

3 Draw a pictogram to show the information.

4 Write 5 questions about your pictogram for a partner.

Challenge

a Copy and complete this frequency table for children in your class.

b Copy and complete the pictogram to show the information.

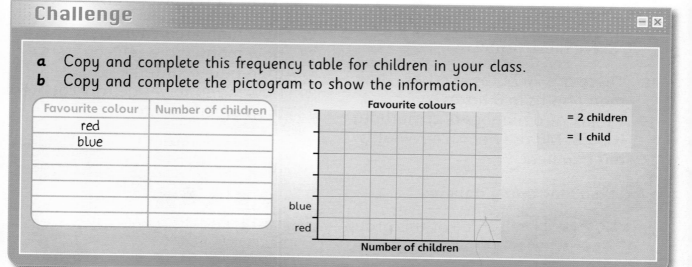

Favourite colour	Number of children
red	
blue	

Favourite colours

= 2 children

= 1 child

blue

red

Number of children

Can you solve a problem by organizing data in frequency tables and pictograms?

A Write the next 3 numbers in each sequence.

1 44 54 64 74

2 11 21 31 41

3 16 36 76 66

4 131 121 111 101

B Find how much is left.

5 Simon has £165 and spends £10.
6 Andy has £620 and spends £100.
7 Kate has £862 and spends £300.

C Answer these.

8 3 × 7 = ◼
9 3 × ● = 27
10 10 × 4 = ◖
11 ▲ × 7 = 70
12 11 × 10 = ●
13 9 × 5 = ⬡

D Find the cost of:

£1·20

80p

14 2 lollies
15 2 ice-creams
16 2 ice-creams and 1 lolly
17 5 ice-creams.

E Solve these problems.

18 There are 20 bulbs in a box. How many bulbs in 6 boxes?
19 I think of a number and multiply it by 6. My answer is 24. What is my number?

F Find how many ants in:

20 $\frac{1}{5}$ of this group

21 $\frac{1}{3}$ of this group.

G Find what fraction of each shape is yellow.

22

23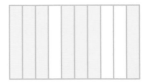

H Find the answer.

24 $\frac{3}{4}$ of 8
26 $\frac{3}{5}$ of 15
28 $\frac{7}{10}$ of 20
25 $\frac{2}{3}$ of 12
27 $\frac{4}{5}$ of 30

I Find the missing number.

29 7 + ★ = 20
31 9 − ◼ = 2
30 42 + 10 = ●
32 2 + ✸ + 9 = 17

J Find the difference between:

33 601 and 597
35 904 and 899
34 502 and 496
36 404 and 395.

K Look at the pictogram.

37 How many red counters?
38 How many more red counters than blue counters?
39 How many fewer yellow counters than green counters?

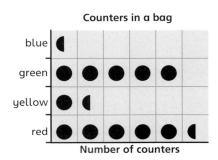

Counters in a bag

● = 2 counters
◖ = 1 counter

blue
green
yellow
red

Number of counters

A Find which is less.

| 1 | 27 |

1 42 or 27   4 60 or 49
2 38 or 83   5 33 or 17
3 53 or 49   6 91 or 89

B Find which is more.

| 7 | 96 |

7   69 or 96   10 60 or 39
8   53 or 39   11 91 or 72
9   17 or 11   12 80 or 99

C Name who is in each position in the race.

Alice Dot Sally Jess Mo Tessa

| 13 | Sally |

13 3rd   16 6th
14 4th   17 5th
15 1st   18 2nd

D Write the colour of the 17th bead in each pattern.

| 19 | red |

19

20

21

22

E Find which is more.

23 247 or 302   25 426 or 601
24 361 or 602   26 199 or 720

F Find which is heavier.

27 3 kg or 2·5 kg   29 10·5 kg or
28 8·5 kg or 9 kg   11 kg

Challenge   — ×

Use number cards 1 to 9 and a large copy of this grid. Shuffle the cards. Place the top 6 cards in order on the grid. If your number is larger than the machine number, score a point. If not, the machine scores a point.
Have more turns.
Can you reach 10 points before the machine?

Beat The Machine!

Your number   **Machine number**

| 1st card | 2nd card | 3rd card | | 4th card | 5th card | 6th card |

Can you understand and use the vocabulary of comparing and ordering numbers including ordinal numbers?

A Make the largest number with the digits.

1	4 9 2	5	2 9 6
2	3 7 4	6	2 3 7
3	8 5 1	7	4 5 8
4	6 1 3		

1 9 4 2

B Make the smallest number with the digits.

8	1 9 6	12	6 2 1
9	7 1 5	13	1 8 5
10	2 4 3	14	6 2 9
11	3 4 7		

8 1 6 9

C Write in order, smallest first.

15 1 4 6, 2 6 5, 5 6 2

15 265, 562, 146

16 423, 172, 365   19 235, 523, 152

17 401, 140, 104   20 961, 109, 901

18 662, 556, 656   21 335, 355, 353

D Round the number of stamps to the nearest 10.

22

Phil Latterly
48 stamps

24

Penny Black
32 stamps

23

Ivor Rarewon
96 stamps

25

Frank Ing
25 stamps

E Round to the nearest 10.

26	68	29	86	32	29
27	33	30	47	33	15
28	24	31	62	34	75

Challenge

Play with a partner. Use number cards 1 to 9 and 2 sets of 8 counters.
Take turns. Shuffle the cards. Place the top 2 cards to make a 2-digit number .
Round your number to the nearest 10.
If your answer is on the grid, cover it with a counter.
The first to have 8 counters on the grid is the winner.

20	30	80	50
40	10	90	60
30	40	80	70
60	90	10	100

Can you compare two 3-digit numbers and say which is more or less? Can you round any 2-digit number to the nearest 10?

Place value

A Find which colour of wool measures about these lengths.

1 6 cm	2 5 cm	3 9 cm	4 8 cm	5 5·5 cm

B Guess the length of each line. Then measure to the nearest centimetre.

6 _____

7 _____

8 _____

9 _____

> 6 Guess... Measure 6 cm

C Find how much these weigh.

10 the potatoes   11 the brick   12 the apples

D Find how much juice is in each jug.

13   14   15

E Guess which number the arrow is pointing to on each number line. Explain your answer.

16 0 _____ 100

17 0 _____ 100

18 0 _____ 100

19 0 _____ 100

Challenge ▭ ☒

a Find five objects in your classroom that you think weigh about $\frac{1}{2}$ kg.

b Weigh each object.

c Find which objects weigh:
• less than $\frac{1}{2}$ kg • more than $\frac{1}{2}$ kg.

d Order the objects, lightest first.

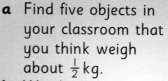

A Find the missing number.

1. 3 + ★ + 7 = 16
2. 4 + 5 + 6 = ▨
3. 2 + 7 + 8 = ★
4. 5 + 4 + ▨ = 14
5. 8 + 3 + 7 = ●
6. 4 + ● + 6 = 18
7. 3 + 2 + 8 = ●
8. 16 + 7 = ●
9. 15 + 8 = ▧
10. 18 + 6 = ◗

1 6

11. 16 + 5 = ▲
12. 14 + 9 = ◖
13. 17 + 6 = ●
14. 3 + 9 + 6 = ✷
15. 5 + 4 + 9 = ⬟
16. 6 + 3 + 8 = ◆
17. 7 + 2 + 9 = ✦

B Add the 4 numbers on each string.

18 21

18. 6 — 3 — 7 — 5
19. 4 — 7 — 4 — 6
20. 2 — 6 — 7 — 8
21. 8 — 9 — 3 — 1
22. 12 — 3 — 5 — 7
23. 14 — 2 — 7 — 6
24. 16 — 2 — 8 — 5

C Answer these. Show your working.

25   38 + 2 + 7 = 40 + 7 = 47

25. 38 + 9
26. 46 + 8
27. 65 + 9
28. 26 + 7
29. 48 + 6

30. 87 + 8
31. 44 + 8
32. 56 + 7
33. 85 + 9

D Answer these.

34   45

34. 28 + 17
35. 36 + 18
36. 65 + 16
37. 55 + 17
38. 37 + 16

39. 45 + 17
40. 32 + 19
41. 64 + 18
42. 57 + 16

Challenge

Play with a partner. Use number cards 1 to 11 and 2 sets of twelve counters. Take turns. Shuffle the cards. Turn over the top 3 cards. Add the 3 numbers. If your answer shows in one of the boxes cover it with a counter. The first to have 3 counters in a box wins the game.

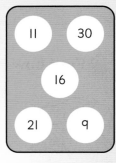

11   30
16
21   9

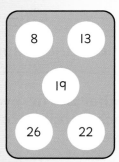

8   13
19
26   22

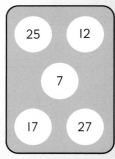

25   12
7
17   27

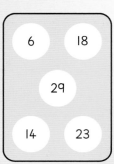

6   18
29
14   23

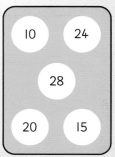

10   24
28
20   15

Can you add 4 single-digit numbers mentally and partition into 5 and a bit to add 6, 7, 8 or 9?

A   Answer these.

1   37 + 26   5   65 + 27
2   45 + 28   6   35 + 28
3   35 + 37   7   25 + 37   9   25 + 28
4   45 + 36   8   55 + 29   10   75 + 18

1 63

B   Solve these problems.

11   A tower is 25 cm high. If an extra 17 cm is added, how high will the tower be?

12   There are 45 counters in a bag. If 19 more counters are added, how many counters will be in the bag?

13   When 2 pieces of wood are placed end to end the total length is 54 cm. If one piece of wood is 15 cm long, how long is the other piece?

C   Find the total of the 4 numbers in:

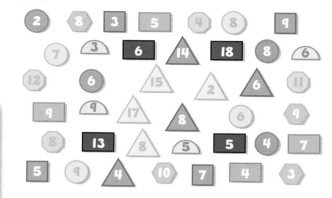

14   the red circles
15   the blue squares
16   the orange hexagons
17   the pink rectangles
18   the yellow circles
19   the orange octagons
20   the pink semi-circles
21   the blue triangles
22   the black rectangles
23   the yellow triangles.

Challenge

Work out the distance a snail crawls if it goes from:

a   A to B to C to D to E
b   B to G to E to C to D
c   L to J to I to H to G
d   B to E to G to F to A
e   J to E to G to F to B
f   H to J to K to E to D
g   D to C to E to H to I
h   D to E to L to I to J
i   I to L to E to H to F.

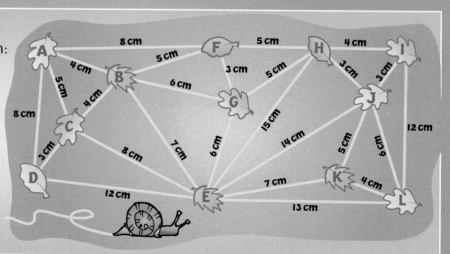

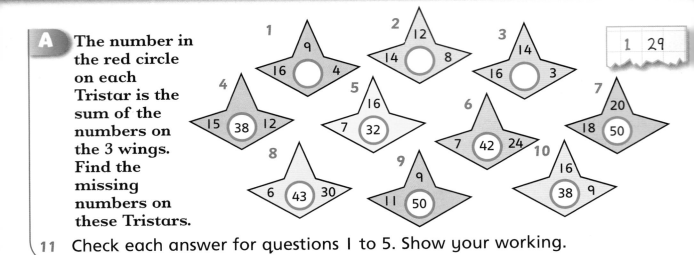

A The number in the red circle on each Tristar is the sum of the numbers on the 3 wings. Find the missing numbers on these Tristars.

1. 9, 16, 4
2. 12, 14, 8
3. 14, 16, 3
4. 15, 38, 12
5. 16, 7, 32
6. 7, 42, 24
7. 20, 18, 50
8. 6, 43, 30
9. 9, 11, 50
10. 16, 38, 9

1 | 29

11 Check each answer for questions 1 to 5. Show your working.

B The number in the yellow circle on each Quadstar is the total of the numbers on the 4 wings. Find the missing numbers on these Quadstars.

12 | 29

12. 5, 17, ○, 3, 4
13. 8, 39, 11, 17
14. 12, 14, 50, 9
15. 17, 55, 13, 16
16. 19, 22, 68, 11
17. 6, 19, 61, 17
18. 32, 80, 17, 19
19. 17, 61, 6, 29
20. 18, 18, 59, 18
21. 27, 99, 25, 33

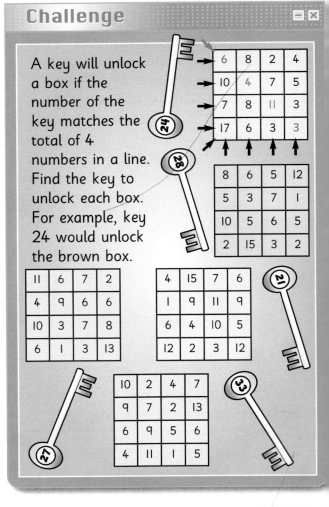

Challenge

A key will unlock a box if the number of the key matches the total of 4 numbers in a line. Find the key to unlock each box. For example, key 24 would unlock the brown box.

Can you check calculations by adding in a different order?

A **Write a number sentence to show how you solved each problem.**

1 Boxes hold 6 eggs. How many eggs are there in 5 boxes?

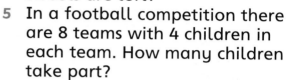

2 Polly buys a drink for 50p and a chocolate bar for 26p. How much does she spend?

3 There are 28 children in a class. 9 of them have blue eyes. How many do not have blue eyes?

4 There are 40 sweets in a bag. If Bill eats half of them, how many sweets are left?

5 In a football competition there are 8 teams with 4 children in each team. How many children take part?

6 Bella's mother gave her 25p and her father gave her 46p. How much has she in total?

B **Solve these problems. Show your working.**

7 Charlie has a bunch of grapes. He eats $\frac{1}{4}$ of them. If there were 24 grapes on the bunch, how many does Charlie eat?

8 Badges cost 8p. If Sally buys 10 badges, how much does she spend?

9 Jack has 35p. He spends 17p and is then given another 50p. How much does he have now?

10 Amy has £5. She buys a notepad for £1·50 and some envelopes for £2·40. How much money has she left?

11 Class 3M is trying to raise £100 for charity. In the first week they raised £35 and in the second week £48. How much money do they still need to raise?

12 There are 52 people on a train. At Greenford Station 24 people get off and 17 people get on. How many people are on the train now?

Challenge

— ☒

a Write 2 one-step problems for your partner. One problem should be easy, the other one difficult.

b Write 2 two-step problems for your partner. One should be easy, the other should be **very** difficult.

Can you choose and use appropriate operations to solve word problems?

53

A Write as pounds.

1 £1·4·5

1 145p   4 316p
2 225p   5 460p   7 806p   9 964p
3 462p   6 309p   8 742p

B Find the total cost of the toys.

10 a bat and ball and a trumpet

10 £9·90

11 a yo-yo and skates
12 a skateboard and a car
13 a Snakes and Ladders game and a ball
14 a car, a doll and a yo-yo
15 2 balls and a skateboard

C Find how much change from £10 if you buy:

16 £3·50

16 a trumpet
17 a doll
18 a bat and ball
19 a Snakes and Ladders game
20 a yo-yo
21 2 balls and a doll.

D Solve these problems.

22 Which 3 toys could you buy for £5?
23 Which 3 toys would cost exactly £37·50?
24 Write 5 different sets of three toys that you could buy for £9 or less.
25 How many yo-yos could you buy with £10?

E Find the change:

26 £2·13

26 from £5 when you spend £2·87
27 from £4 when you spend £3·53
28 from £7 when you spend £6·13
29 from £10 when you spend £6·66
30 from £5 when you spend £1·89.

Challenge ⊟☒

Work out how you can spend each exact amount of money in Toy World. For example, with £11·40 you can buy a bat and ball, a yo-yo and a trumpet.

a £25·50
b £7·60
c £19
d £14·80
e £36·20
f £6·10
g £14·40

 Can you solve word problems including finding totals and giving change?

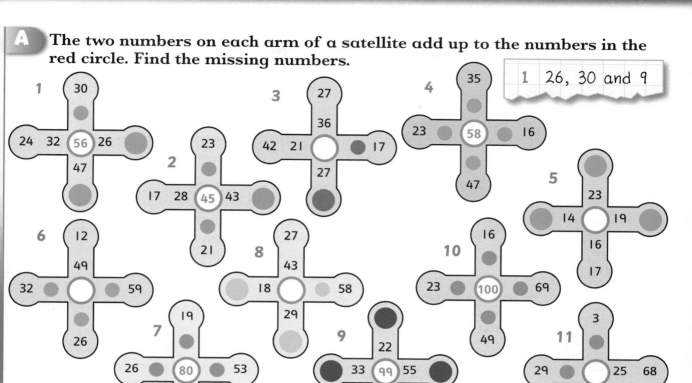

A The two numbers on each arm of a satellite add up to the numbers in the red circle. Find the missing numbers.

1 26, 30 and 9

1
30
24 32 56 26
47

2
17 28 45 43
21

3
27
36
42 21 ○ 17
27

4
35
23 ● 58 ● 16
47

5
23
14 ○ 19
16
17

6
12
49
32 ● ○ ● 59
26

7
19
26 ● 80 ● 53
62

8
27
43
18 ● ○ ● 58
29

9
22
● 33 99 55 ●
44

10
16
23 ● 100 ● 69
49

11
3
29 ● ○ ● 25 68
47

B Find the change from £20 when you buy 3 items costing:

12 £4·67, £2·80, £3·46

13 £2·45, £3·64, £1·86

14 £4·96, £3·27, £11·15

15 £5·26, £3·85, £10·07

16 £6·62, £4·53, £2·97

17 £8·99, £6·98, 46p.

Challenge ▢ ✕

A Chinese restaurant wants to offer 10 different meals costing between £16 and £20.
Each meal must have 1 starter, at least 2 main courses and at least 1 extra item.
Make up 8 different meals. Find the cost of each meal.

~China Inn~

Starter
Hot and sour soup £3·00
Pancake rolls £4·00
Prawn toast £3·80
Chicken soup £2·70

Main course
Crispy duck £7·60
Chicken chop suey £5·60
Pork chow mein £5·10
Sizzling beef £7·50
Spare ribs £6·80

Extras
Noodles £1·80
Rice £1·35
Beansprouts £3·20
Fried vegetables £3·80

Can you choose the appropriate number operations and ways of calculating to solve problems?

55

You need:
- a partner
- 2 sets of 25 counters

Take turns to answer a question and place a counter on the ball next to it.

Find the answer in the grid and cover it with another counter.

The winner is the first to have three counters together in a straight line on the grid.

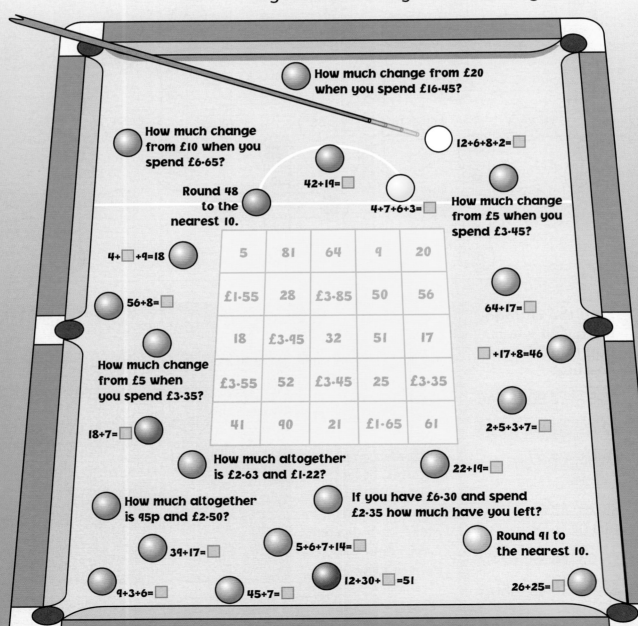

How much change from £20 when you spend £16·45?

12+6+8+2=☐

How much change from £10 when you spend £6·65?

42+19=☐

4+7+6+3=☐

Round 48 to the nearest 10.

How much change from £5 when you spend £3·45?

4+☐+9=18

5	81	64	9	20
£1·55	28	£3·85	50	56
18	£3·95	32	51	17
£3·55	52	£3·45	25	£3·35
41	90	21	£1·65	61

56+8=☐

64+17=☐

☐+17+8=46

How much change from £5 when you spend £3·35?

18+7=☐

2+5+3+7=☐

How much altogether is £2·63 and £1·22?

22+19=☐

How much altogether is 95p and £2·50?

If you have £6·30 and spend £2·35 how much have you left?

39+17=☐

5+6+7+14=☐

Round 91 to the nearest 10.

9+3+6=☐

45+7=☐

12+30+☐=51

26+25=☐

A Name each 2D shape.

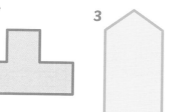

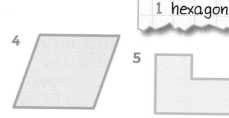
1 hexagon

4

5

B

Use these 2D shapes: a square, a rectangle and 2 triangles. The sides of the square, each side of both triangles and the longer side of the rectangle must be the same length.

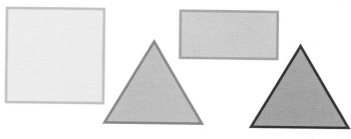

6 Choose 2 of your shapes. Put them together to make a new shape.
7 Draw your new shape.
8 Name the new shape.

9 Make, draw and name 10 more shapes in this way.

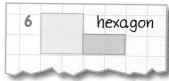
6   hexagon

C

Use 4 squares, all the same size. If you place them side by side you can make different shapes.

10 Make as many different shapes as you can.
11 Draw your shapes on squared paper.

Challenge

Use cubes. Fit cubes face to face to make each of these shapes:

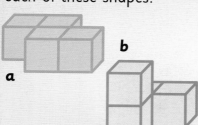

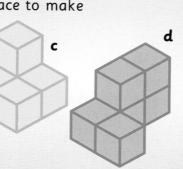

a

b

c

d

How many different shapes can you make using 4 cubes? For example,

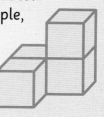

Can you make and describe shapes and patterns and relate solid shapes to pictures of them?

57

A Find the compass direction shown by each arrow.

1 black arrow
2 red arrow
3 blue arrow
4 orange arrow

1 north

B Find which direction they are sailing.

5 south

5 blue ship
6 red ship
7 brown ship
8 yellow ship

C You are in the lighthouse. Write which direction you will look to see:

9 the brown ship   10 the red ship.

D You are on the yellow ship. Write which direction you will look to see:

11 the red ship   12 the brown ship.

E Look at the grid. Give directions for:

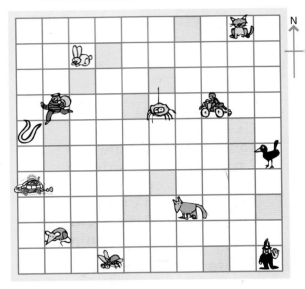

13 4 squares east, 2 squares north, 3 squares east, 1 square north

13 the police car to catch the motorbike
14 the spider to catch the fly
15 the cat to catch the mouse
16 the policeman to catch the robber
17 the blackbird to catch the worm
18 the fox to catch the rabbit.

Challenge

Copy this grid onto squared paper.
Answer these to find a secret message.
a Write L 4 squares north of ●
b Write N 3 squares east of ●
c Write D 2 squares south of ●
d Write L 4 squares east of ○

e Write E 1 square south of ●
f Write O 4 squares south of ●
g Write E 3 squares west of ●
h Write W 1 square east of ○

Can you read and begin to write the vocabulary of direction?

Map of underground caves

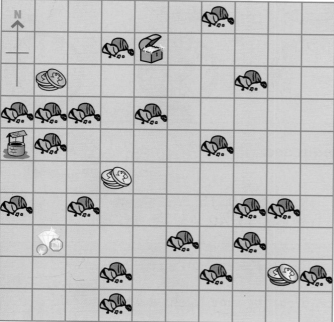

A The robots can only make right-angled turns. Give directions for each robot so that they do not bump into the rocks.

> 1 3 squares west, 1 square south, 2 squares west, 4 squares south, 2 squares west

1 Robot 1 to the gold coins
2 Robot 2 to the treasure chest
3 Robot 3 to the bronze coins
4 Robot 4 to the silver coins
5 Robot 5 to the jewels
6 Robot 6 to the secret well

B Answer this.

7 Write directions for a partner for 5 different robot journeys.

Challenge

On the grid, follow each set of secret directions. Write the letters you reach. What is in the box?
a From B3: 2E, IN, 2E, 2S
b From AI: 3N, 5E, IS, 3W
c From E6: 5S, 3W, 2N, IW
d From F5: 3W, IN, 2E, 5S
e From B2: IS, IE, 4N, IW
f From FI: 5W, 5N, 5E
g From E4: 3W, 2N, IW, 4S
h From D2: 4N, IE, 2S, 2W

a S

	A	B	C	D	E	F
6	B	B	C	D	M	O
5	T	S	R	G	U	F
4	A	H	S	X	W	Y
3	I		C	D	N	E
2	R	E	Z	K	Q	S
I	L	V	A	J	S	P
	A	B	C	D	E	F

Can you make and use right-angled turns and use the four compass points?

59

A Write these times.

 1

 3

 5

 7

1 quarter past eight

2 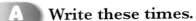 (blank)

4 (blank)

6 (blank)

8 (blank)

9

B Write the next 3 numbers in each sequence.

10 35, 40, 45

10 15, 20, 25, 30, ⬤, ⬤, ⬤

11 25, 30, 35, 40, ◼, ◼, ◼

12 10, 15, 20, 25, ⬟, ⬟, ⬟

13 0, 5, 10, 15, ✳, ✳, ✳

14 30, 35, 40, 45, ◾, ◾, ◾

Use 12 blank clock faces. On each clock face, draw the time to show when you do these things.

a
wake up

d
arrive at school

g
go for lunch

j
have tea

b
have breakfast

e
start lessons

h
afternoon lessons

k **?**
something you do in the evening

c
leave for school

f
go to play

i
leave school

l
go to bed

Can you read the time to 5 minutes on an analogue clock?

A   Find how long it takes for the minute hand to move from A to B.

1 A   B
`1  15 minutes`

2   A B

3  A B

4  A B

B   Write each time in 2 ways.

5
`5  quarter to 6`
`   5:45`

6    8   10

7   9   11

C   Write each time.
`12  5:35`

12 10 minutes later than [5:25]

13 5 minutes earlier than [6:20]

14 20 minutes earlier than [4:55]

15 $\frac{1}{2}$ hour earlier than [10:20]

16 25 minutes later than [9:50]

17 20 minutes earlier than [11:10]

18 $\frac{3}{4}$ hour later than [6:30]

Challenge   ▬ ☒

a On blank clock faces copy and complete this time chain for the television programmes.

News → Wildlife on 10 →

What's On TV   31st February

Channel 10

7:00	News
7:30	Wildlife on 10
8:15	Big Sister
9:00	Weather
9:05	Boss and Company
9:40	Stargazers
9:55	Pop goes the Otter
10:20	Film of the Night
11:55	Late Music

b Make a time chain for programmes on your own television channel. Put in the programmes you enjoy at the times you want to watch them.

Can you read the time to 5 minutes on a 12-hour digital clock?

A

Find out the time spent on each activity.

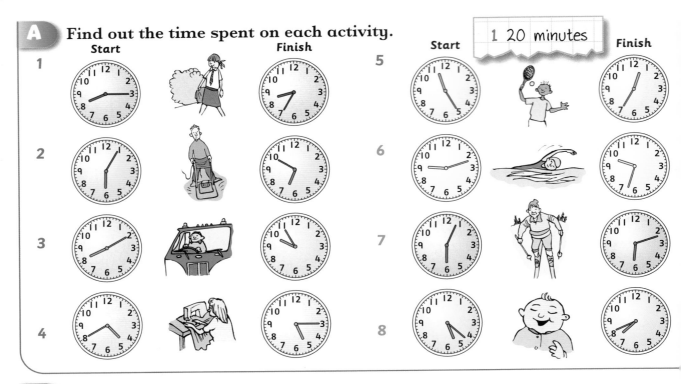

Start   Finish   Start   1 20 minutes   Finish

1

2

3

4

5

6

7

8

B Answer these.

9 It takes Tess Coe 35 minutes to do her shopping. If she finishes at 11:20, at what time does she start?

10 Holly Berry gardens for 1 hour and 20 minutes. If she finishes at 1:05, at what time does she start?

11 Delia Baker wants her cake to be cooked by 3:45. If the cake takes 55 minutes to cook, at what time must she put it in the oven?

12 Ivor Motor starts driving at 6:40. If he drives for 53 minutes, at what time does he stop?

Challenge

a Write the digital times for this astronaut's journey to Mars.

b Make a time chain like this for your own journey to Mars.

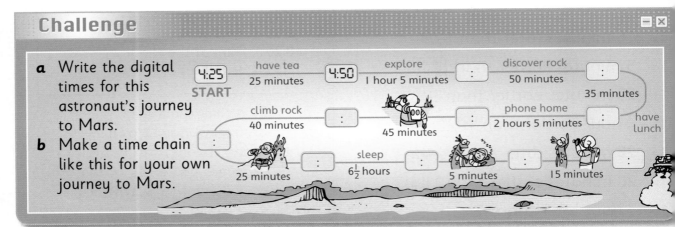

4:25 START — have tea 25 minutes — 4:50 — explore 1 hour 5 minutes — [:] — discover rock 50 minutes — [:]

climb rock 40 minutes — [:] — 45 minutes — [:] — phone home 2 hours 5 minutes — [:] — have lunch

[:] — 25 minutes — [:] — sleep 6½ hours — [:] — 5 minutes — [:] — 15 minutes — [:]

35 minutes

Can you solve problems involving time?

When the hands are drawn correctly on each clock they point at the red letters.

On each clock, work out the position of the minute hand and then the hour hand.

Write the letter each hand points to. (Use a ruler to find them.)

Find the secret message.

Answer the question.

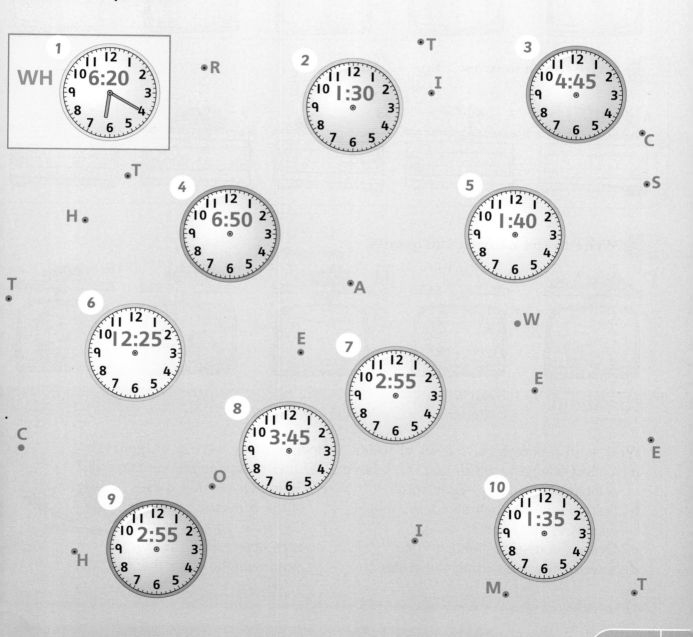

A Write to the nearest kilogram.

1 2 kg

 1

 2

 3

 4

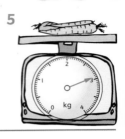 5

B Write to the nearest ½ kg.

 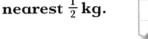

6 1½ kg

 6

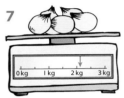 7

 8

 9

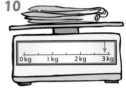 10

C Write to the nearest 100 grams.

11 300 g

 11

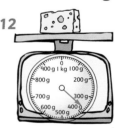 12

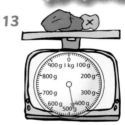 13

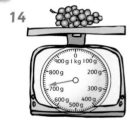 14

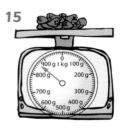 15

Challenge — x

Work with a partner. Use a set of scales.
a Collect 8 objects which you think have a mass of less than 1 kg in total.
b Say how much each object roughly weighs to the nearest 100 g.
c Order the objects, lightest first.
d Check each mass using the scales.

How accurate were your guesses?
Did you order the objects correctly?
e Give your partner a list of the 8 masses.
f Can your partner match each object with the correct mass without using the scales?

Can you read and begin to write the vocabulary related to mass and read scales?

A

Write what the mass of each object is in kilograms and grams.

1 4 kg 500 g

1    $4\frac{1}{2}$ kg

2    $2\frac{1}{2}$ kg

3   5 kg

4    $1\frac{1}{2}$ kg

5   1 kg

6    $\frac{1}{2}$ kg

C

Find which 2 objects below have a mass of exactly:

12   $1\frac{1}{2}$ kg

13   1 kg

14   $\frac{1}{2}$ kg

15   750 g

16   600 g   17   1100 g   18   1 kg 50 g.

12 parcel and bottle

B

Write in order, lightest first.

7   1000 g, $1\frac{1}{2}$ kg, 2 kg, 2500 g

7   2 kg, 2500 g, $1\frac{1}{2}$ kg, 1000 g

8    $1\frac{1}{2}$ kg, 3000 g, $2\frac{1}{2}$ kg, 500 g

9   2500 g, 3 kg, 2 kg, 2·5 kg

10   3·5 kg, 3000 g, $2\frac{1}{2}$ kg, $4\frac{1}{2}$ kg

11   500 g, 1 kg, 800 g, $1\frac{1}{2}$ kg

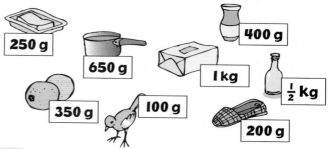

250 g   650 g   400 g   1 kg $\frac{1}{2}$ kg   350 g   100 g   200 g

D

Find which 3 objects have a mass of exactly:

19   1 kg   20 $1\frac{1}{2}$ kg   21   800 g.

Challenge

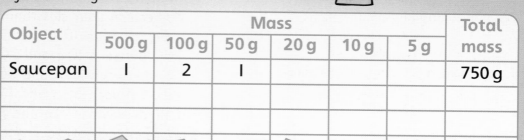

Use balance scales and a set of weights.
a   Choose 5 objects from your classroom.
b   Weigh each object carefully
c   Copy and complete this table.

Object	Mass						Total mass
	500 g	100 g	50 g	20 g	10 g	5 g	
Saucepan	1	2	1				750 g

Can you measure and compare using kg and g and do you know the relationship between them?

65

A Solve these problems.

1 Pens weigh 25 g. How much do 8 pens weigh?

`1 200 g`

2 Tubs of butter weigh 250 g. How much do 4 tubs weigh?

3 4 rulers each weigh the same. Together they weigh 64 g. How much does each ruler weigh?

4 If a spoon weighs 50 g, how many spoons will weigh $\frac{1}{2}$ kg?

5 A box of matches weighs 10 g. How much do 100 boxes weigh?

6 For a curry, 100 g of rice is needed for each person. How many people can be served using 1 kg of rice?

7 In her bag Sharon has $\frac{1}{2}$ kg of onions, 700 g of apples, a tin of soup weighing 500 g and a packet of tea weighing 80 g. What do all the items weigh?

8 Postman Nat, Postman Matt and Postman Pat are delivering these parcels. Nat carries 4 parcels weighing a total of 37 kg. Matt delivers 3 parcels weighing a total of 23 kg and Pat delivers 3 parcels weighing a total of 21 kg 500 g. Work out which parcels each postman carries.

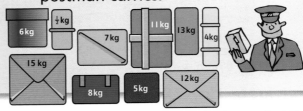

B Rewrite this recipe so that you can serve:

Chicken Korma – for 4 people

30 g butter
1 medium onion
2 cloves of garlic
250 g of natural yoghurt
500 g chicken
50 g cashew nuts
2 tablespoons chopped coriander
200 g rice
spices

9 2 people
10 8 people
11 20 people.

Challenge — ☒

Use balance scales and weights. Find 3 objects in your classroom that weigh:

a less than 10 g
b between 10 g and 20 g
c between 20 g and 50 g
d between 50 g and 100 g
e between 250 g and 500 g
f between 500 g and 1 kg.

Can you choose appropriate number operations and calculation methods to solve measurement word problems?

Review 3

unit **7**   **Spring** term

A Answer these.

1 What 2 even numbers lie between 17 and 21?
2 What number is half-way between 9 and 13?
3 Write 2 numbers that lie between 29 and 32.

B Write in order, largest first.

4 136, 263, 162, 621, 123
5 345, 435, 543, 535, 553
6 111, 109, 911, 901, 910
7 246, 264, 216, 241, 214

C Round to the nearest 10.

8 67   10 81   12 14
9 73   11 18   13 66

D Answer these.

14 56 + 7   17 67 + 19   20 54 + 37
15 69 + 8   18 33 + 18   21 65 + 29
16 46 + 15   19 46 + 25

E Find how much change from £10 when you spend:

22 £8·27   24 £4·06
23 £7·92   25 £1·92.

F Find the missing numbers.

26 68 + ⬤ = 100
27 46 + ⬡ = 53
28 47 + ◖ = 83
29 ✱ + 24 = 99

G Find the direction of each object from the lighthouse.

30 the yacht
31 the shark
32 the swimmer
33 the ship

H Write as digital clock times.

34
37
35
38
36
39

I Write to the nearest ½ kg.

40
42
41
43

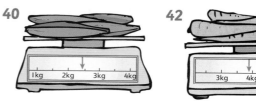

A
Centimon counts in hundreds. Write the first 6 numbers in each count.

1 300, 400, 500, …
2 100, 200, …
3 0, 100, 200, …
4 250, 350, …
5 233, 333, …

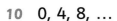

1 300, 400,
   500, 600,
   700, 800

B
Trimon counts in threes. Write the first 10 numbers in each count.

6 3, 6, 9, …
7 12, 15, 18, …
8 5, 8, 11, …
9 14, 17, 20, …

C
Quadmon counts in fours. Write the first 10 numbers in each count.

10 0, 4, 8, …
11 6, 10, 14, …
12 21, 25, 29, …
13 33, 37, 41, …

D
Pentamon counts in fives. Write the first 10 numbers in each count.

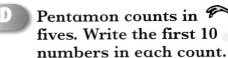

14 0, 5, 10, …
15 25, 30, 35, …
16 1, 6, 11, …
17 29, 34, 39, …

E
Write the rule for each sequence.

18 Count back in steps of 3.

18 59 – 56 – 53 – 50 – 47 – 44
19 41 – 45 – 49 – 53 – 57 – 61
20 43 – 38 – 33 – 28 – 23 – 18
21 58 – 61 – 64 – 67 – 70 – 73
22 100 – 96 – 92 – 88 – 84 – 80
23 61 – 66 – 71 – 76 – 81 – 86

F
Find the missing numbers in each sequence. Write the rule.

24 12, 28
    Count on in steps of 4.

24 4, 8, ▲, 16, 20, 24, ▲
25 42, 45, ⬣, 51, 54, 57, ⬣
26 59, ▮, 49, 44, 39, ▮, 29
27 18, 15, 12, ▮, 6, 3, ▮
28 67, 71, ▮, ▮, 83, 87, 91

Challenge

Which of these numbers will be in each count?   56   61   60   52

a 26 – 31 – 36 – 41 –
b 77 – 75 – 73 – 71 – 69 –
c 15 – 20 – 25 – 30 –

d 100 – 98 – 96 – 94
e 4 – 6 – 8 – 10 – 12
f 96 – 92 – 88 – 84 – 80
g 250 – 240 – 230 – 220 –

Can you describe and extend number sequences?

A Write the missing numbers for each sequence. Work out the rule.

1 24, ⬛, 30, 33, ⬛, ⬛
2 68, 🥔, 88, 🥔, 108
3 ⚫, 325, ⚫, 525, 625
4 59, 🌙, 49, 44, 🌙
5 100, ⬛, 94, ⬛, 88
6 0, ⭐, 10, ⭐, 20
7 32, ✿, ✿, 23, 20
8 93, 91, ✳, 87, ✳
9 ⬛, 63, 67, ⬛, 75
10 132, ⬛, 112, ⬛, 92

> 1 27, 36, 39
> Count on in steps of 3.

B Write a sequence with these numbers in it. Write the rule for each sequence.

11 8 and 17
12 9 and 17
13 10 and 35
14 6 and 21
15 1 and 16
16 9 and 21
17 16 and 28
18 3 and 28

> 11 5, 8, 11, 14, 17, 20
> Count on in steps of 3.

C Write 'odd' or 'even' for each number.

> 19 odd

19 261
20 207
21 537
22 269
23 316
24 604
25 948
26 621
27 410
28 308

D Using the digits 1, 5 and 2, write:

29 3 different odd numbers
30 2 different even numbers.

Challenge ▬ ⊠

Can you find:

a any 2 odd numbers that add together to make an odd number

b any 2 even numbers that add together to make an odd number

c an odd number that is not 1 less than an even number

d an even number that is not 1 more than an odd number

e an odd and an even number that add together to make an even number?

Make a statement about:

f the sum of 2 odd numbers

g the sum of 2 even numbers

h the sum of an odd and an even number

i what happens when you add 1 to an odd number

j what happens when you subtract 1 from an even number.

k Give 5 examples to match each statement.

A Solve these problems.

1 Each parcel weighs a different whole number of kilograms. The total weight of the red parcel and the yellow parcel is 11 kg. The total weight of the yellow parcel and the blue parcel is 7 kg. The total weight of all 3 parcels is 15 kg. What does each parcel weigh?

2 Liz, Beth and Eddy have been given some pound coins. Together, Liz and Eddy have £12. Together, Beth and Liz have £14. Together, Beth and Eddy have £8. How much money does each person have?

3 After a walk for charity, Classes 3, 4, 5 and 6 collect £66. The total for Class 3 and Class 4 is £39. The total for Class 3 and Class 5 is £36. If Class 6 collects £15, how much do Classes 3, 4 and 5 collect?

Challenge

In the yellow box find:
a 2 odd numbers with a sum of 88
b 3 even numbers with a sum of 102
c an odd and an even number with a difference of 19
d a 2-digit number greater than 40. The sum of the digits is 9, and the difference between them is 3.
e 3 numbers with a sum of 77. The second number is half the first and the third number is half the second.
f 3 odd numbers with a sum greater than 60 but less than 70.

4		25	
11	12		15
54	44		81
63		17	23
	22		

Can you solve mathematical problems or puzzles?

A Answer these.

1   Add 2, 7 and 12.
2   Add 6, 5 and 11.
3   6 plus 13 plus 4
4   Find the sum of 5, 9 and 8.
5   Subtract 40 from 70.
6   Find how many less 9 is than 16.
7   23 subtract 6
8   Find the total of 6, 7, and 8.
9   Find the difference between 11 and 20.

`1  21`

10   Find how many more 15 is than 8.
11   Find what number you must take from 30 to leave 11.

12   62 − 7
13   51 − 8
14   64 − 5
15   92 − 7

16   62 − ⬟ = 57
17   41 − ⬤ = 38
18   53 − ✸ = 47
19   82 − ◖ = 75

B The village archers use a 100 square for a target. Work out the total scored by:

`20  19 + 35 + 51 = 105`

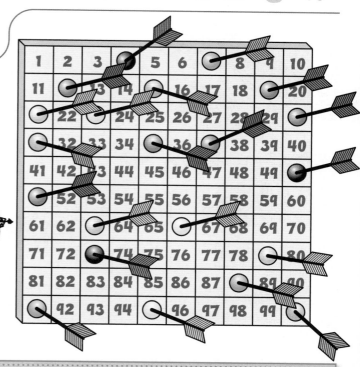

20   the blue arrows
21   the red arrows
22   the black arrows
23   the green arrows
24   the orange arrows
25   the pink arrows
26   the yellow arrows.

Challenge

Each archer has 3 arrows. If all 3 arrows score:
a   find the lowest possible score
b   find the highest possible score
c   find as many different scores as you can.
d   Write your own target numbers.
e   Answer questions a, b and c with your target numbers.

Can you add three 2-digit numbers using apparatus or informal methods?

71

A Write the missing numbers.

1   12 + ● + 5 = 23
2   7 + ■ + 11 = 30
3   16 + ■ + 4 = 31

4   8 + 9 + ✳ = 25
5   ● + 11 + 12 = 40
6   5 + 6 + ▲ = 17

1 6

7   4 + 19 + 6 = ⬡
8   15 + 9 + ✿ = 31

B Find the total cost of these items.

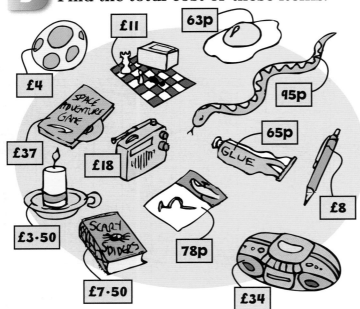

£11   63p   £4   95p   £37   65p   £18   £8   £3·50   78p   £7·50   £34

9   a chess set, a pen and a radio
10   Space Adventure, a CD player and a chess set
11   a CD player, a radio and a book
12   a ball, a candle and a book
13   a snake, a plastic egg and a nail in finger
14   glue, a snake and a plastic egg
15   a pen, a CD player and a radio
16   a chess set, a radio and Space Adventure
17   2 candles, 2 books and a pen
18   3 chess sets, 3 pens and a ball

Challenge   ⊟☒

Play with a partner. Use number cards 1 to 9 and a large copy of this grid.
Take turns. Shuffle the cards. Place the top 6 cards on the grid.
Add up your 3 numbers.
The player with the higher total scores a point.
First to 5 points wins.

| 1st card | 2nd card | ✚ | 3rd card | 4th card | ✚ | 5th card | 6th card |

Can you partition into tens and units and recombine?

A Solve these problems.

1   In a money box there are
37 10p coins, 25 20p coins and 17 £1
coins. Find the total number of coins.

2   I think of a number and subtract 16.
My answer is 36. What is my
number?

3   Alex pays 93p using 5 coins. Which
5 coins does she use?

4   Jim Bow buys a bag of
40 buns at the zoo. He
gives 11 buns to one
elephant and 16 to another. How
many buns has he left?

5   Jeff buys 2 books for £10. If one
book costs £3·50, what is the cost of
the other book?

6   There are 35 fish in a
tank. If 18 more fish
are put in and 26 are taken out,
how many fish are left in the tank?

7   There are 91 melons on display in a
supermarket. 53 are bought and
another 26 are put on display. How
many are on display now?

8   Daisy has 56 flowers. She gives 8
flowers to each of her 3 friends.
How many flowers has she left?

9   A squirrel has 95 acorns.
He eats 26 acorns and
gives 17 to his friend. He
then collects another 22 acorns.
How many acorns has he now?

10 In a horse jumping event Jan scores
142 points, but she loses 36 points
by knocking down fences. She also
loses 17 points for riding too slowly.
What is her final score?

11 A builder has 565 bricks. If he uses
123 on a wall and 158 for a
barbecue, how many bricks are left?

Challenge

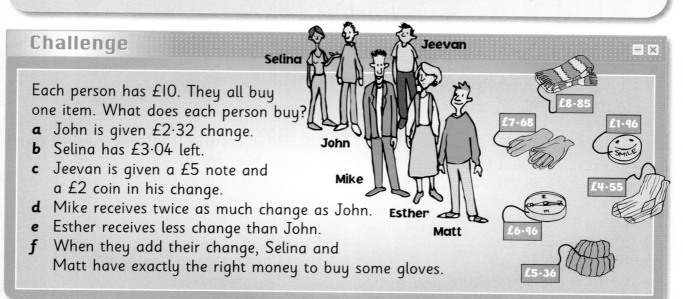

Each person has £10. They all buy
one item. What does each person buy?
a   John is given £2·32 change.
b   Selina has £3·04 left.
c   Jeevan is given a £5 note and
a £2 coin in his change.
d   Mike receives twice as much change as John.
e   Esther receives less change than John.
f   When they add their change, Selina and
Matt have exactly the right money to buy some gloves.

Selina   Jeevan   John   Mike   Esther   Matt

£8·85
£7·68
£1·96
SMILE
£4·55
£6·96
£5·36

Can you choose appropriate number operations and calculation
methods to solve money or 'real-life' word problems with two steps?

73

What's his message?

You need: ● 21 counters

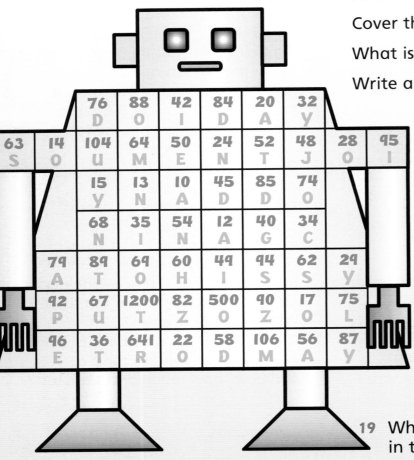

76 D	88 O	42 I	84 D	20 A	32 Y		

63 S	14 O	104 U	64 M	50 E	24 N	52 T	48 J	28 O	95 I
		15 Y	13 N	10 A	45 D	85 D	74 O		
		68 N	35 I	54 N	12 A	40 G	34 C		
79 A	89 T	69 O	60 H	49 I	94 S	62 S	29 Y		
92 P	67 U	1200 T	82 Z	500 O	90 Z	17 O	75 L		
96 E	36 T	641 R	22 O	58 D	106 M	56 A	87 Y		

Answer each question.

Find the answers on the robot.

Cover them with counters.

What is the hidden message?

Write an answer to the message.

10 What is the sum of 27 and 36?

11 How many grams is 1 kg 200 g?

12 If knives weigh 50 g, how many knives will weigh 1 kg?

13 How many grams make $\frac{1}{2}$ kg?

14 $16 + ◖ + 7 = 35$

15 What is the next number in this sequence? 100, 97, 94, 91, ✴

16 $46 + 32 + 17$

17 $6 + 15 + 8$

18 $32 + 49 + 13$

19 Which is the largest odd number in this group?

47 68 79 84 33 44 96 51

20 Which is the smallest even number in this group?

19 86 72 64 57 100 33 51 35

21 Which odd number between 80 and 100 is missing from this group?

91 83 99 95 97 89 93 87 81

1 What is the next number in this sequence? 68, 64, 60, 56, ●

2 $76 - 8$

3 $8 + 7 + ▮ = 32$

4 What is the next number in this sequence? 86, 91, 96, 101, ■

5 $43 - 9$

6 $26 + 15 + 28$

7 $▮ + 9 + 12 = 31$

8 $16 + ◖ + 11 = 40$

9 What is the largest number you can make using the digits 1, 6 and 4?

A Answer these.

1 Share 20 between 2.
2 Share 16 between 2.
3 Divide 10 by 2.
4 Find how many each if 9 cows are shared equally among 3 farmers.
5 Divide 6 by 3.
6 Find how many £2 coins you get for £14.
7 Find how many is half of 18.

`1  10`

8 60 ÷ 10
9 Find how many fives in 20.
10 Find how many is half of 60.
11 Find how many tens in 70.
12 40 ÷ 2

C Answer these.

`17  8`

17	80 ÷ 10	20	90 ÷ 10	23	100 ÷ 10
18	20 ÷ 4	21	16 ÷ 2	24	32 ÷ 4
19	25 ÷ 5	22	27 ÷ 3	25	500 ÷ 100

B Write 2 multiplication facts and 2 division facts for each array.

13 ● ● ● ●
    ● ● ● ●
    ● ● ● ●

```
13  4 × 3 = 12
    3 × 4 = 12
    12 ÷ 3 = 4
    12 ÷ 4 = 3
```

14 ○ ○ ○
    ○ ○ ○
    ○ ○ ○
    ○ ○ ○

16 ○ ○ ○ ○ ○
    ○ ○ ○ ○ ○
    ○ ○ ○ ○ ○

15 ● ● ● ● ● ● ● ● ●
    ● ● ● ● ● ● ● ● ●
    ● ● ● ● ● ● ● ● ●

D Solve these problems.

26 In a bag of 9 counters, 1 counter in every 3 is yellow. How many yellow counters are there?
27 24 peppers are packed in boxes of 4. How many boxes can be filled?
28 There are 25 children in the drama club. One child in every 5 is in Year 3. How many Year 3 children are there?

Challenge — ×

Follow the correct answers. Who is Croaker visiting?

15÷3 5 3
60÷10 6
9
32÷4 8 6
40÷5 9 8 7
28÷4 6
18÷3 9 6
40÷10 5 4
36÷4 8
25÷5 5 7
35÷5 5 7
21÷3 6 7
36÷4 9 8
700÷100 17 7
800÷100 8 18
16÷4 9 6 4
27÷3 8 9
50÷10 5 10

Do you understand division and recognize that division is the inverse of multiplication?

75

A — Double each number.

1 50

1 25
2 45
3 200
4 350
5 15
6 65
7 16
8 17
9 35
10 18
11 150

D — Find one quarter.

31 6

31	24	34	20	37 32
32	16	35	8	38 12
33	28	36	40	39 36

B — Halve each number.

12 35

12 70	15 34	18 38	
13 26	16 30	19 500	21 50
14 36	17 800	20 90	22 900

E — Write 2 multiplication facts and 2 division facts that link these numbers.

40 3, 15, 5
41 2, 10, 5
42 4, 12, 3
43 50, 10, 5
44 4, 5, 20
45 2, 4, 8
46 5, 100, 500

40 $3 \times 5 = 15$
$5 \times 3 = 15$
$15 \div 3 = 5$
$15 \div 5 = 3$

C — Copy and complete.

23 $4 \times 5 = 20$

23 4×5
24 4×3
25 4×4
26 4×7
27 2×4
28 10×4
29 4×9
30 4×8

Challenge

Look at Ellen's homework.
Use multiplication to check her divisions.
Which answers are wrong?
Write the correct answers for the questions that are wrong.

a $35 \div 5 = 9$ **e** $18 \div 3 = 5$ **i** $45 \div 5 = 7$
b $32 \div 4 = 7$ **f** $90 \div 10 = 9$ **j** $40 \div 5 = 6$
c $60 \div 10 = 6$ **g** $36 \div 4 = 8$ **k** $27 \div 3 = 7$
d $18 \div 2 = 9$ **h** $15 \div 3 = 6$ **l** $24 \div 4 = 6$

Can you check answers to division problems by using multiplication?

A Solve these problems.

1 How many children can be given 5 sweets from a packet of 35 sweets?

2 How many each when 27 fish are divided equally among 3 fishermen?

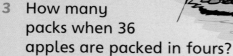

3 How many packs when 36 apples are packed in fours?

4 If beads cost 4p each, how many beads can be bought for 32p?

5 A washing machine can wash a total of 5 large towels. How many washes will be needed for 45 towels?

6 There are 30 children in a class. Three children sit at each table. How many tables are needed?

7 Mrs Peel bought 24 oranges. A quarter of them were not ripe. How many oranges were not ripe?

8 Three men share £150 equally. How much does each man get?

B Find how many each.

9 6 children have an equal share of 30 comics.

10 8 spiders have an equal share of 32 flies.

11 7 birds have an equal share of 56 worms.

12 6 goats have an equal share of 36 turnips.

13 9 gardeners have an equal share of 45 plants.

14 8 whales have an equal share of 72 fish.

Challenge

Use this secret code to answer the questions.

a Draw a picture of a … . $40 \div 4 = $ ★,
 ▲ $\div 10 = 10$, $32 \div 4 = $ 🍎

b Do you like to eat … ? $27 \div 3 = $ 🍌,
 $\frac{1}{2}$ of 32, $10 \times 10 = $ ◯ , $\frac{1}{2}$ of 50, ▪ $\div 4 = 5$, $45 \div 5 = $ 🍎

c Write the number … .half of 70, ◯ $\div 2 = 7$, $30 \div 3 = $ ▪,
 $24 \div 3 = $ ★, $27 \div $ ⬡ $= 9$

d Write division problems as clues to spell out the word GREAT.

Y	3	L	20
W	4	K	24
U	5	I	25
T	8	H	28
S	9	G	32
R	10	F	35
P	12	E	36
O	14	C	45
N	16	B	50
M	18	A	100

Can you choose appropriate number operations and calculation methods to solve money or 'real-life' word problems with two steps?

77

A   **What fraction of each shape is coloured?**

1

2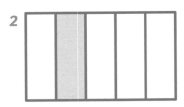

3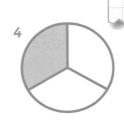

4

5

6

7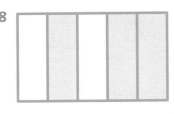

8

9

$1 \frac{1}{4}$

B   **Find in which colour seed tray:**

10   $\frac{1}{2}$ of the plants are showing

11   $\frac{1}{5}$ of the plants are showing

12   $\frac{7}{10}$ of the plants are showing

13   $\frac{4}{5}$ of the plants are showing

14   $\frac{3}{3}$ of the plants are showing

15   $\frac{3}{10}$ of the plants are showing

16   $\frac{3}{5}$ of the plants are showing.

Challenge   — ✕

Make 5 copies of this shape on squared paper.
- **a** Colour half of the first shape to form the letter I.
- **b** Colour $\frac{3}{5}$ of the second shape to form the letter L.
- **c** Colour $\frac{4}{5}$ of the third shape to form the number 3.
- **d** Colour $\frac{1}{2}$ of the fourth shape to form the number 7.
- **e** Colour $\frac{8}{10}$ of the fifth shape to form the letter E.

L   I   E   3   7

Can you begin to recognize simple equivalent fractions, e.g. $\frac{5}{10}$ is equivalent to $\frac{1}{2}$, $\frac{5}{5}$ to 1 whole?

A Use squared paper.

1 Draw 5 copies of this rectangle. Colour $\frac{1}{2}$ of each rectangle in a different way.

2 Draw 5 copies of this rectangle. Colour $\frac{2}{5}$ of each rectangle in a different way.

3 Draw 5 copies of this square. Colour $\frac{1}{4}$ of each square in a different way.

Challenge　⊟☒

Use 16 counters.
Shapes d and k have the same fraction shaded. Cover them with counters.
Find other pairs of shapes with the same fraction shaded. Cover them with counters.
Which shape is not covered with a counter?

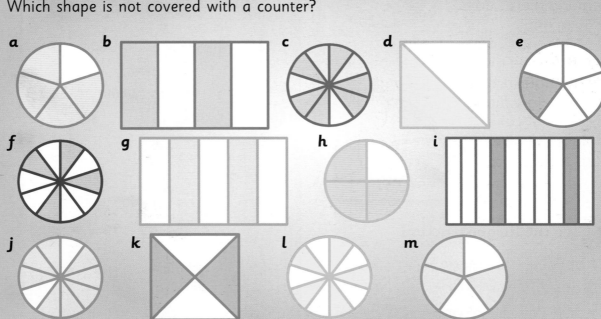

A Find how many:

1 2

1 quarters make one half
2 tenths make one fifth
3 tenths make one half
4 thirds make one whole
5 tenths make three fifths
6 quarters make one whole
7 fifths make one whole.

B Solve these problems.

8 Bill cuts his pizza into quarters. He gives half of the pizza to Zoe. How many pieces does he give to her?

9 Raj cuts his pizza into tenths. He gives Suzy $\frac{2}{5}$ of the pizza. How many pieces does Suzy get?

10 Mrs Flower cuts a cake into tenths. She gives Jack Flap half of the cake. How many pieces of cake does she give to Jack?

C Give the larger fraction.

11 $\frac{2}{5}$ or $\frac{1}{2}$ 15 $\frac{1}{10}$ or $\frac{1}{4}$

11 $\frac{1}{2}$

12 $\frac{3}{10}$ or $\frac{1}{2}$ 16 $\frac{3}{5}$ or $\frac{1}{2}$

13 $\frac{1}{5}$ or $\frac{1}{4}$ 17 $\frac{3}{4}$ or $\frac{3}{5}$

14 $\frac{1}{3}$ or $\frac{1}{5}$ 18 $\frac{7}{10}$ or $\frac{4}{5}$

Challenge

At each treasure chest, follow a fraction with the same value. What treasure do you find?

START

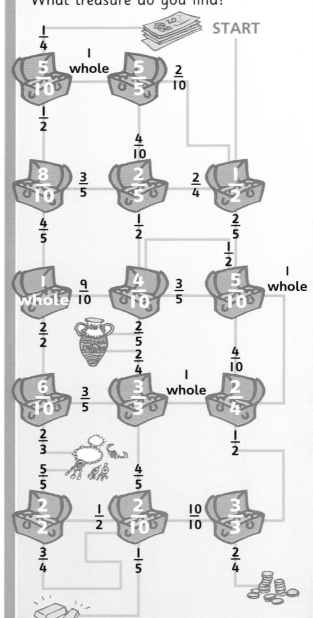

Can you begin to recognize simple equivalent fractions?

8

Write the numbers missing from each section of each target in this order:

a purple   **c** pink   **e** yellow   **g** brown

b orange   **d** grey   **f** red   **h** blue.

A Look at the block chart on minibeasts.

  1 3

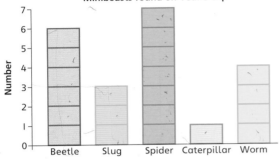

Minibeasts found on Year 3 trip

1 How many slugs were found?
2 How many beetles were found?
3 How many worms were found?
4 How many more spiders than worms were found?
5 How many fewer caterpillars than spiders were found?
6 How many more beetles than caterpillars were found?
7 How many slugs and worms were found in total?
8 How many spiders and beetles were found in total?
9 How many minibeasts were found?

B Look at the bar chart on goal scorers.

10 5

10 How many goals did Annie score?
11 Who scored most goals?
12 Who scored fewest goals?
13 Who scored the same number of goals as Dave?
14 How many more goals than Mike did Fred score?
15 How many fewer goals than Dave did Salma score?
16 How many children scored more than 3 goals?
17 How many goals were scored?
18 What fraction of the goals did Fred score?

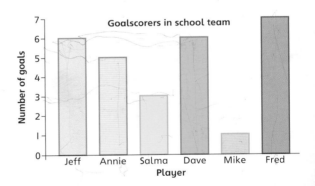

Goalscorers in school team

Challenge

Copy and complete this bar chart for flowers in the garden.

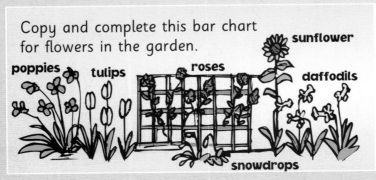

poppies tulips roses sunflower daffodils snowdrops

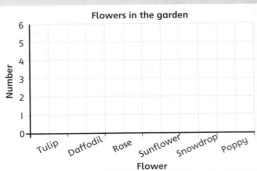

Flowers in the garden

Can you solve a problem by organizing and interpreting data in bar charts — intervals labelled in ones?

A Look at the bar chart.

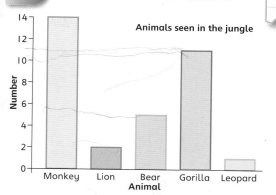

Animals seen in the jungle

1 How many lions were seen?
2 How many gorillas were seen?
3 How many monkeys were seen?
4 How many leopards were seen?
5 How many bears were seen?
6 How many more gorillas than lions were seen?
7 How many fewer lions than monkeys were seen?
8 How many monkeys and gorillas were seen in total?
9 What is the total number of animals seen?

B Look at the fish tank.

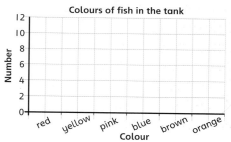

Colour of fish	Number
red	
yellow	
pink	
blue	
brown	
orange	

10 Copy and complete this table to show the colours of fish in the tank.

C Use the table with the numbers of fish.

11 Copy and complete this bar chart.

Colours of fish in the tank

Challenge

a Find the number of letters in the first name of each child in your class.
b Copy and complete the table.
c Copy and complete this bar chart.

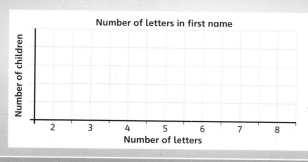

Number of letters in first name

Number of letters in first name	Number of children
2	
3	
4	
5	
6	
7	
8	

Can you solve a problem by organizing and interpreting data in bar charts – intervals labelled in twos?

83

A
Use the information on these bar charts. Find each alien's name.

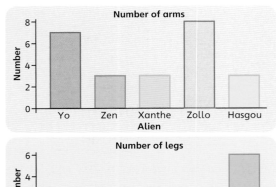

Number of arms

Number of eyes

1

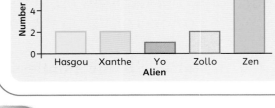

Number of legs

2

3

B
Find out the birthday month of each child in your class.

4

5

6 Complete this table with your results.

Birthday month	Number of children
January	
February	
March	

7 Draw a bar chart to show your results. Give your graph a title.

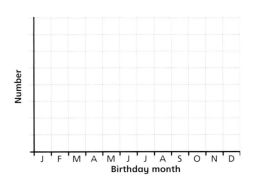

Number

J F M A M J J A S O N D
Birthday month

Challenge

Write 5 questions for a partner about this bar chart.

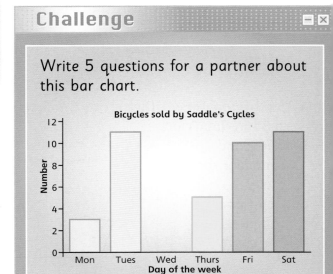

Bicycles sold by Saddle's Cycles

Number

Mon Tues Wed Thurs Fri Sat
Day of the week

Can you solve a problem by organizing and interpreting data in bar charts?

A Write odd or even for each number.

1	243	3	742	5	307
2	613	4	800	6	420

B Give the missing numbers for each sequence. Write the rule.

7  36 – 40 – 44 – ◯ – 52 – 56 – ◯ – 64

8  26 – 23 – ◯ – 17 – 14 – 11 – ◯ – 5

9 96 – ◯ – ◯ – 66 – 56 – 46 – 36 – 26

10  7 – 12 – ◯ – ◯ – 27 – 32 – 37 – 42

C Write the missing numbers.

11   7 + ■ + 12 = 25
12   14 + 3 + ● = 26
13   6 + 18 + 7 = ⬟
14   16 + 8 + ★ = 31
15   ● + 6 + 7 = 24
16   15 + ■ + 4 = 30

D Answer these.

17	20 ÷ 5	22	27 ÷ 3
18	18 ÷ 2	23	700 ÷ 100
19	60 ÷ 10	24	80 ÷ 10
20	25 ÷ 5	25	24 ÷ 4
21	45 ÷ 5	26	24 ÷ 3

E Double each number.

27	25	32	350
28	18	33	17
29	14	34	250
30	45	35	75
31	150		

F Halve each number.

36	24	39	36	42	700
37	80	40	400	43	28
38	60	41	30	44	90

G Find how many:

45   quarters make one half
46   fifths make one whole
47   tenths make one half
48   tenths make four fifths
49   thirds make one whole
50   halves make one whole.

H Look at the bar chart.

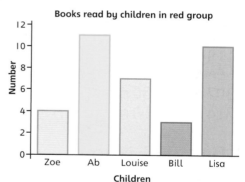

Books read by children in red group

51   How many books did Zoe read?
52   How many books did Louise read?
53   How many more books did Lisa read than Bill?
54   How many fewer books did Zoe read than Ab?
55   How many books did Ab and Louise read in total?
56   Find the total number of books read.

A Write the number that is 1 less.

1	328	5	899
2	423	6	461
3	197	7	300
4	906	8	420

9 750

1 327

B Write the value of the red digit.

10	437	14	684
11	256	15	137
12	819	16	427
13	609	17	394

18 432

10 thirty

C Find which is longer.

19	210 m or 120 m
20	126 m or 206 m
21	324 m or 423 m
22	119 m or 911 m
23	654 m or 645 m
24	302 m or 230 m
25	714 m or 709 m

19 210 m

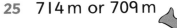

D Find which is heavier.

26	402 kg or 249 kg
27	345 kg or 453 kg
28	207 kg or 199 kg
29	810 kg or 188 kg
30	751 kg or 749 kg

E Write an even number between these numbers.

31	163 and 167
32	149 and 153
33	260 and 264
34	899 and 905
35	193 and 196
36	98 and 101
37	639 and 642

31 166

F Write an odd number between these numbers.

38	367 and 372
39	557 and 561
40	498 and 501
41	99 and 102
42	638 and 641
43	399 and 402

Challenge

Use number cards 1 to 9 and a large copy of these grids.
Shuffle the cards. Place the first 6 cards on the grids.
Write your 2 numbers. Which number is larger? Write 2 odd numbers and 2 even numbers that come between your 2 numbers.
Have 5 more turns.

First number

| 1st card | 2nd card | 3rd card |

Second number

| 4th card | 5th card | 6th card |

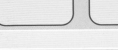

Can you compare two 3-digit numbers, say which is more or less and give a number that lies between them?

A Round each amount to the nearest £100.

1 £380   3 £946   5 £650
2 £715   4 £532

B Round the number of football fans to the nearest 100.

	Team	Fans
6	Rovers	582
7	United	450
8	City	964
9	Rangers	513
10	Town	685

C Write these distances in order, shortest first.

11 865 miles 685 miles 901 miles
843 miles 209 miles

12 326 km 143 km 430 km
279 km 327 km

13 596 miles 602 miles 562 miles
499 miles 506 miles

14 350 km 530 km 305 km
503 km 335 km

15 646 miles 664 miles 644 miles
666 miles 466 miles

D Write the amounts in order, smallest first.

16 £721 £712 £271 £217 £227
17 £606 £566 £605 £556 £655
18 £942 £899 £901 £189 £819
19 £427 £742 £447 £724 £398
20 £616 £761 £617 £176 £167

Challenge ▬ ☒

Play with a partner. Use number cards 1 to 9, a dice and 2 counters. Place your counters on START. Take turns. Shuffle the cards. Lay out the top 3 to make a 3-digit number. Roll the dice and count around the track. If your number matches the statement score a point.

For example, 326 less than 412
score 1 point

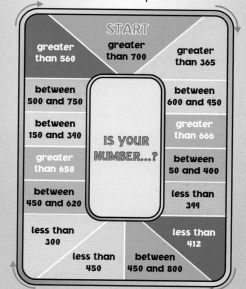

The first to 10 points is the winner.

Can you round a 3-digit number to the nearest 100?

A Write the missing numbers in each sequence.

1 459 465 467

B Look at the number line. Find which colour arrow points to each number.

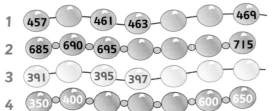

1 457 461 463 469
2 685 690 695 715
3 391 395 397
4 350 400 600 650

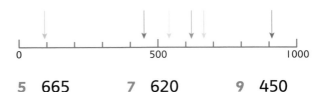

| 5 | 665 | 7 | 620 | 9 | 450 |
| 6 | 910 | 8 | 91 | 10 | 540 |

C Find roughly what these objects weigh.

11 129g

11
12
13
14
15
16
17

D Round to the nearest 100.

18 6400

| 18 | 6432 | 20 | 7780 | | | 23 | 1850 | 25 | 4850 |
| 19 | 6275 | 21 | 3284 | 22 | 4726 | 24 | 3027 | 26 | 6502 |

Challenge — ☒

Play with a partner. Use number cards 1 to 9, a large copy of this grid and two sets of 12 counters.

Take turns. Shuffle the cards. Lay out the top 3 to make a 3-digit number. Round your number to the nearest 100.
If your answer is on the grid, cover it with a counter.
The first with 3 counters together in a straight line is the winner.

500	600	100	100	300
400	800	500	700	800
700	200	300	900	200
600	500	100	100	400

Can you identify unlabelled divisions on a number line or measuring scale?

A   Answer these.

1   12 + 7 + 8
2   9 + 11 + 7
3   4 + 13 + 7
4   6 + 17 + 4
5   8 + 9 + 12
6   7 + 13 + 9
7   14 + 11 + 6

B   Find the difference between these numbers.

8   15 and 7
9   12 and 8
10   13 and 6
11   18 and 9
12   12 and 5
13   16 and 7
14   11 and 6
15   13 and 8

8   8

C   Answer these.

16   136 + 40
17   128 + 30
18   117 + 50
19   145 + 40
20   162 + 30
21   126 + 70
22   119 + 60

16   176

D   Write 2 multiples of 10 to complete each number sentence.

23   140 + 90 + 70 = 300

23   140 + ■ + ● = 300
24   130 + ◗ + ● = 400
25   120 + ◗ + ◖ = 350
26   90 + ✸ + ● = 250
27   210 + ★ + ▲ = 400
28   160 + ✸ + ◼ = 320

E   Find the difference between these numbers.

29   32 and 6
30   47 and 8
31   32 and 5
32   41 and 6
33   33 and 8
34   54 and 9
35   82 and 7
36   64 and 6

29   26

F   Copy and complete.

37

+	2	3	4	5
2	4	5	6	7
3	5			
4		7		
5			9	

39

+	1	2	4	5
3				
4				
7				
9				

38

+	1	2	3	4
5				
6				
7				
8				

40

+	3	4	7	9
2				
6				
8				
9				

Challenge   − ×

Make as many different totals as you can, using 3 of these numbers.

12   9

7   8   15

For example, 12 + 7 + 8 = 27

A Find how many more than:

1 6 is 38
2 4 is 47
3 8 is 49
4 7 is 68

5 3 is 45
6 2 is 63
7 4 is 76.

1 32

B Write 2 numbers with a difference of:

8 32 7

8 **25**
9 **30**
10 **20**

11 **13**
12 **32**
13 **51**

14 **45**
15 **29**
16 **63**

C Answer these.

17 282

17 273 + 9
18 264 + 11
19 328 − 9
20 426 + 11
21 637 − 11
22 412 − 9
23 843 + 9

24 641 − 11
25 724 − 9
26 185 + 9
27 686 − 11

D Copy and complete.

28 68 + 29
29 85 − 19
30 66 − 31
31 47 + 29
32 56 + 39
33 73 − 39
34 55 − 31
35 40 − 11
36 37 + 49
37 18 + 49
38 63 − 29
39 39 + 41
40 62 − 41

28 68 + 29 = 97

Challenge

a Copy and complete this giant addition square.
b Write about any patterns you can find.

+	1	2	3	4	5	6	7	8	9	10
1										
2						8				
3			6							
4										
5										
6										
7										
8									17	
9										
10										

A
Work out each set of missing numbers.

1   34   44   54   64   74

1
$26 + 8 =$ ★
$26 + 18 =$ ▣
$26 + 28 =$ ★
$26 + 38 =$ ▮
$26 + 48 =$ ◼

2
$85 - 7 =$ ⬤
$85 - 17 =$ ⬤
$85 - 27 =$ ◼
$85 - 37 =$ ◖
$85 - 47 =$ ✳

3
$27 + 6 =$ ◔
$27 + 16 =$ ⬤
$27 + 26 =$ ✳
$27 + 36 =$ ⬤
$27 + 46 =$ ★

4
$7 + 5 =$ ✴
$70 + 50 =$ ▲
$700 + 500 =$ ▰

5
$5 + 6 =$ ⬤
$50 + 60 =$ ▰
$500 + 600 =$ ▰

6
$19 + 27 =$ ⬤
$29 + 27 =$ ★
$39 + 27 =$ ◖
$49 + 27 =$ ⬤
$59 + 27 =$ ◗

7
$16 + 9 =$ ▰
$16 + 19 =$ ⬤
$16 + 29 =$ ◖
$16 + 39 =$ ◖
$16 + 49 =$ ⬤

B
Answer these.

8   485

8   $400 + 85$
9   $500 + 62$
10   $85 + 700$
11   $18 + 600$
12   $700 + 29$
13   $81 + 500$
14   $300 + 27$

C
Use 18 counters. Answer each question. Cover the answers on the woodland trail. Who reaches the tree house?

15   $74 + 12$
16   $63 + 14$
17   $43 + 16$
18   $26 + 72$
19   $81 + 16$
20   $42 + 34$
21   $32 + 25$
22   $26 + 53$
23   $32 + 37$
24   $31 + 43$
25   $12 + 87$
26   $23 + 31$
27   $22 + 17$
28   $24 + 22$
29   $22 + 27$
30   $15 + 65$
31   $33 + 45$
32   $27 + 61$

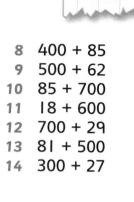

33   Write a set of subtraction clues for Mike to reach the tree house.

Challenge ▢ ✕

Write sets of clues to make trails for Max and Millie to reach the tree house.

A Answer these.

1 46 + 30
2 53 + 30
3 47 + 20
4 64 + 30
5 17 + 60
6 74 − 30
7 61 − 40
8 98 − 50
9 300 + 500
10 300 + 400

| 1 | 76 |

11 600 + 200
12 800 − 400
13 500 + 400
14 700 − 200
15 200 + 500
16 800 − 700

B Write the missing number.

17 300 + 800 =
18 700 + 500 =
19 600 + 800 =
20 900 + 400 =
21 1500 − 700 =
22 ● − 600 = 800
23 1200 − ★ = 600
24 500 + ● = 1100
25 800 + 800 = ●
26 1700 − ✱ = 900

| 17 | 1100 |

C Answer each question. Show your working.

27 magpie

46 + 27

28 hawk
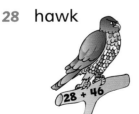
28 + 46

29 crow

29 + 52

30 goldfinch

36 + 58

31 pigeon

19 + 16

32 thrush
19 + 18

33 yellowhammer
65 + 63

34 blackbird

26 + 25

35 wren
28 + 45

36 cormorant

59 + 81

37 woodpecker
73 + 73

Challenge

Find which bird has the perch with:
a the largest answer
b the smallest answer
c the answer nearest to 50
d an answer that is a multiple of 10
e an answer between 120 and 135
f an answer that is double the answer on the wren's perch
g an answer between 79 and 84
h an answer that is half the answer on the hawk's perch.

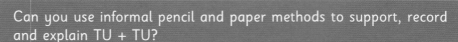

A Answer these. Show your working.

1 139 + 15
2 245 + 38
3 427 + 39
4 143 + 61
5 324 + 85
6 219 + 59
7 64 + 138
8 59 + 160
9 73 + 156

B Find the total money in:

£147 £139 £287 £138 £265

10 the red bag and the yellow bag
11 the blue bag and the orange bag
12 the pink bag and the red bag
13 the yellow bag and the orange bag
14 the blue bag and the yellow bag
15 the orange bag and the pink bag
16 the red bag and the blue bag
17 the blue bag and the pink bag.

Challenge

Play with a partner. Use number cards 1 to 9 and a large copy of these grids.

Take turns. Shuffle the cards. Place 6 cards on the grids.

Total your 2 numbers and write down the total.

The player with the larger total scores a point.

Carry on until 1 player scores 6 points.

First number

| 1st card | 2nd card | 3rd card |

+

Second number

| 4th card | 5th card | 6th card |

Can you use informal pencil and paper methods to support, record or explain HTU + TU and HTU + HTU?

93

A Solve these problems.

1 Joanne writes 235 words and then another 134 words. How many words does she write in total?

2 Charlie swims 185 m and then another 319 m. How far does he swim?

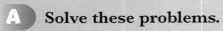

3 Mr Turning drives from London to Edinburgh. Before lunch he drives 186 miles. After lunch he drives 226 miles. How long is the journey?

4 Phil has 483 stamps. He is given another 279 stamps. How many stamps does he have in total?

5 Lily has £426. She is given another £149 and then another £289. How much money does she have now?

6 A train travels from Manchester with 427 people. It makes one stop where 110 people get off and 64 get on. How many people are on the train at the end of the journey?

7 A spider climbs 316 cm from the floor. It falls back 80 cm and then climbs a further 467 cm. How high above the floor is the spider now?

B Look at questions 1, 2, 3 and 4.

8 Check your answers. Show your working.

C Use squared paper.

9 Copy and complete this crossword.

Clues across:
1 537 + 144
3 459 + 216
5 457 + 454
6 258 + 478
8 188 + 259
10 526 + 146
12 89 + 440
14 678 + 210
15 268 + 149
16 155 + 218

Clues down:
1 198 + 449
2 87 + 109
3 266 + 348
4 238 + 299
7 165 + 222
9 369 + 93
10 396 + 268
11 189 + 98
12 418 + 165
13 486 + 467

Challenge ▫ ☒

Write a number story to match each number sentence.

a $57 + 112 = 169$

b $85 + 239 = 324$

c $1400 - 600 = 800$

d $527 + 183 = 710$

e $1400 - 700 = 700$

f $478 + 183 = 661$

Can you choose appropriate number operations and calculation methods to solve money or 'real-life' problems with one or two steps?

Answer the questions in order.

Write the letter from the code bar that is next to your answer.

Follow the secret instructions – don't tell anyone what they are!!

1. Which is the larger number, 268 or 312?

2. Which is the smaller number, 615 or 516?

3. Round 261 to the nearest 100.

4. 11 + 6 + 9

5. 125 + 60

6. Round 749 to the nearest 100.

7. 355 + 445

8. What is the difference between 57 and 9?

9. What is the next number in this sequence: 491, 493, 495, 497, 499, ?

10. 326 + 11

11. 76 − 19

12. 48 + 39

13. 236 − 9

14. 484 − 11

15. 75 −29

16. Round 888 to the nearest 100.

17. 47 + 32

18. 700 + 600

19. 400 + 800

20. 400 + ▲ = 1000

21. 56 + 67

22. 48 + 74

23. 65 + 77

24. 335 + 86

25. 77 + 265

26. 248 + 126

27. 426 + 193

28. 376 + 485

29. 127 + 478

30. 447 + 278

Code bar
answers

185	Y
605	E
79	O
421	I
300	L
57	A
473	E
725	D
800	U
374	I
1200	H
227	H
619	S
312	T
142	F
46	R
342	N
700	O
1300	U
501	T
900	Y
861	H
516	E
123	V
48	R
337	E
600	A
26	L
122	E
87	C

A
Find which object in each pair has the greater capacity.

1    2   3   4

1 bath

B
Is the capacity greater or less than 1 litre?

5   6   7   8   9

5 greater

C
Find how many millilitres of water in each container.

10 700 ml

10	11	12	13
1000 ml 800 ml 600 ml 400 ml 200 ml	1000 ml 800 ml 600 ml 400 ml 200 ml	1000 ml 800 ml 600 ml 400 ml 200 ml	1000 ml 800 ml 600 ml 400 ml

14	15	16	17	18	19
1000 ml 800 ml 600 ml 400 ml 200 ml	1000 ml 800 ml 600 ml 400 ml 200 ml	1000 ml 800 ml 600 ml 400 ml 200 ml	1000 ml 500 ml	1000 ml 500 ml	1000 ml 500 ml

Challenge   — ×

Use a litre measure marked every 100 ml and 10 containers, each with a capacity of less than 1 litre.

a Copy the table.

b List your containers.

c Guess the capacity of each container to the nearest 100 ml.

d Write your guesses in the table.

e Measure the capacity of each container to the nearest 100 ml.

f Find the difference between your guess and the measure.

g Complete the table.

Container	Capacity estimate	measure	difference
	ml	ml	ml
	ml	ml	ml
	ml	ml	ml
	ml	ml	ml
	ml	ml	ml
	ml	ml	ml
	ml	ml	ml
	ml	ml	ml
	ml	ml	ml
	ml	ml	ml

Can you read and begin to write the vocabulary related to capacity and read scales?

A Write the capacity in millilitres.

1 4500 millilitres

1 $4\frac{1}{2}$ l   2 1 litre   3 $\frac{1}{2}$ litre   4 5 l   5 1 l 200 ml   6 $\frac{3}{4}$ l

---

B Find the larger capacity.

9 $\frac{1}{4}$ l or 300 ml   11 1100 ml or 1 l

7 600 ml or $\frac{1}{2}$ l   8 900 ml or 1 l   10 580 ml or $\frac{1}{2}$ l   12 $\frac{3}{4}$ l or 950 ml

---

C Find how many times each container can be filled using 1 litre of water.

13 5 times

13 200 ml   14 250 ml   15 500 ml   16 100 ml   17 50 ml

D Find an object below with a capacity of about:

18 5 litres
19 $\frac{1}{2}$ litre
20 30 litres

21 600 litres
22 5 millilitres
23 1000 millilitres.

Challenge ▭ ✕

Use 6 containers, all with a capacity of less than $\frac{1}{2}$ l, and a litre measure.
a Copy the table.
b Guess how many times each container can be completely filled using 1l of water.
c Write your guess in the table.
d Use a litre of water to check your guesses.
e Complete the table.

Container	Number of fills using 1l of water	
	Estimate	Measure
	fills	fills
	fills	fills
	fills	fills
	fills	fills
	fills	fills
	fills	fills

Can you measure and compare using litres and millilitres and do you know the relationship between them?

97

A Solve these problems.

250 ml   1·5 l

100 ml   5 ml

300 ml   I l

230 ml   385 ml

1 How many cupfuls of water will fill the jug?

2 How many spoonfuls of medicine in a full bottle?

3 Freddie has a litre bottle full of water.
He drinks 250 ml.
How much water has he left?

4 Will the litre measure overflow when 4 full glasses of water are poured in?

5 What is the total capacity of the glass and the cup?

6 350 ml of milk are needed to make one milkshake. How much milk is needed for 3 milkshakes?

7 Jane has 120 ml of medicine. She takes one 5 ml spoonful every day. For how many days can she take the medicine?

8 From a $\frac{1}{2}$ l carton of orange juice, Beth pours 2 drinks of 150 ml. How much juice is left in the carton?

9 Glasses hold 200 ml of lemonade. How many litre bottles of lemonade would you need to buy to fill 27 glasses?

10 A serving of soup is 400 ml. How many people can be served with 4 l of soup?

11 Can a 6 l watering can fill all these containers?

12 You need 100 ml of milk to make a cup of hot chocolate. If milk costs 55p a litre, how much will the milk cost to make 30 cups of hot chocolate?

$\frac{1}{2}$ l   800 ml   2 l

I l 250 ml   1·5 l

Challenge

Use 10 containers, each with a capacity of less than I litre.

YOU CANNOT USE A MEASURE

a List your containers in order of capacity, smallest first.
b Explain how you were able to do this.

 Can you choose appropriate number operations and calculation methods to solve measurement word problems with one or more steps?

A Find which dotted line is the line of symmetry.

1 blue

 1    2   3   4   5

B Copy these patterns on squared paper. Draw 2 more circles on each pattern to make it symmetrical.

6   7   8   9

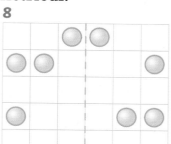

C Find how many lines of symmetry each shape has. Write 0, 1, 2 or more than 2.

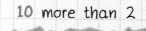
10 more than 2

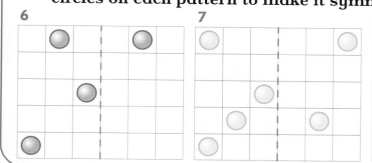

10   11   12   13

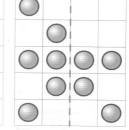

14   15   16   17

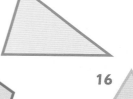

Challenge   − ×

a Draw three half shapes with a line of symmetry. For example,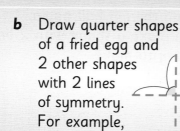

b Draw quarter shapes of a fried egg and 2 other shapes with 2 lines of symmetry. For example,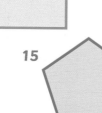

c Can your partner work out what your completed half shapes would be?

Can you identify lines of symmetry in simple shapes and recognize shapes with no lines of symmetry?

99

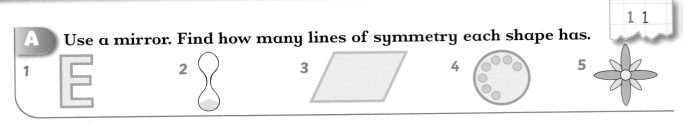

A Use a mirror. Find how many lines of symmetry each shape has.

1   2   3   4   5

B Copy these half shapes and the line of symmetry on squared paper.
Complete each shape.

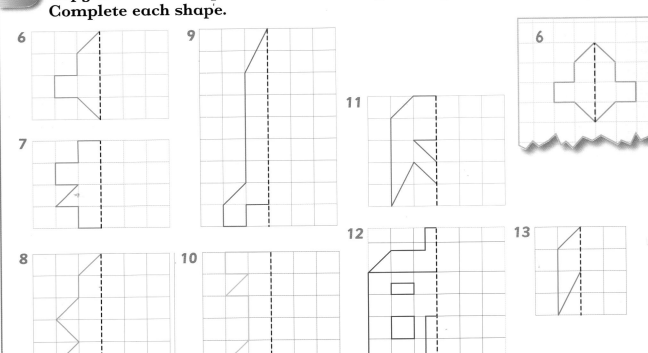

6   9   6

11

7

12   13

8   10

Challenge

Use scrap paper and scissors.
a Fold a piece of paper in half and then in half again.
b Cut a shape from the corner to make a shape with 2 lines of symmetry.
   Cut out a shape in the same way to make:
   c a flower
   d a circle
   e a square.
What other shapes can you make?

Can you identify lines of symmetry and sketch the reflection of a simple shape in a mirror?

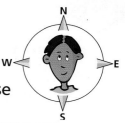

A Vikram is facing north. Find which direction he will face if he turns:

1 I right angle clockwise
2 2 right angles clockwise
3 2 right angles anti-clockwise
4 I right angle anti-clockwise
5 3 right angles clockwise.

B Find which direction the arrow will point after turning:

6 west

6 2 right angles anti-clockwise
7 I right angle clockwise
8 3 right angles anti-clockwise
9 3 right angles clockwise.

C Copy and complete this table. Write how to make each turn.

	You are facing	You turn	You are now facing
	south	2 right angles anti-clockwise	north
10	east		south
11	south		west
12	west		south
13	east		west
14	north		south
15	east		north

Challenge

a Copy the grid onto cm-squared paper. Complete the table to lead the ant from point X to point U.

b An ant with a broken leg can only turn clockwise. Write how this ant can travel from point Z to point S.

Ant facing	Ant turns	Walks forward
north	I right angle clockwise	2 cm
east	I right angle anti-clockwise	2 cm
north	3 right angles anti-clockwise	

c Write how to make 3 more ant journeys.

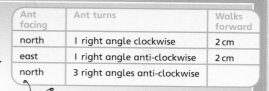

Can you read and begin to write the vocabulary of position, direction and movement?

101

You need:

- a partner
- 2 counters
- 12 cards (3 of each labelled North, South, East and West)
- a dice

Place your counters on START in the middle of the grid.

Shuffle the cards and place them in a pile.

Take turns to roll the dice and turn a card to give a move.

For example, ⚃ | North | means move 4 squares north.

If your move takes you off the board, return to START.

If you land on a yellow square, do what it says.

If it says 'collect 300 ml of water' write down 300 ml.

The first to collect a total of 2 litres or more of water wins the game.

WATER COLLECTION

collect 50 ml of water	take 100 ml of water from your partner		collect 300 ml of water	take another turn		RETURN TO START		collect 150 ml of water
take another turn		collect 50 ml of water			collect 100 ml of water		take another turn	
collect $\frac{1}{4}$ l of water	collect $\frac{1}{2}$ l of water			collect 200 ml of water		W—E (N/S)	collect $\frac{1}{4}$ l of water	
	take another turn		collect 200 ml of water W—E (N/S)				RETURN TO START	collect 100 ml of water
collect 50 ml of water W—E (N/S)			W—E (N/S)	START W—E (N/S)		collect 200 ml of water		take another turn
		collect 150 ml of water		W—E (N/S)	collect 200 ml of water		collect 150 ml of water	
RETURN TO START		take another turn		take another turn		W—E (N/S)		collect $\frac{1}{4}$ l of water
	collect $\frac{1}{2}$ l of water			collect 100 ml of water		collect 300 ml of water		
collect 50 ml of water		RETURN TO START	collect 300 ml of water		take 100 ml of water from your partner		collect $\frac{1}{4}$ l of water	take another turn

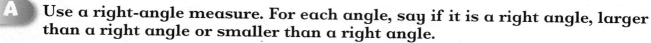

A Use a right-angle measure. For each angle, say if it is a right angle, larger than a right angle or smaller than a right angle.

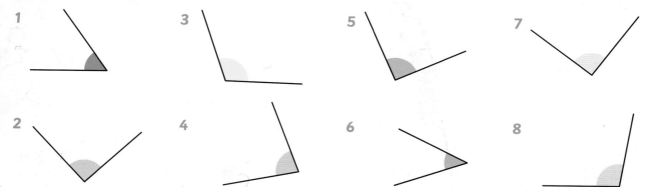

1

3

5

7

2

4

6

8

B Find how many right angles in each shape.

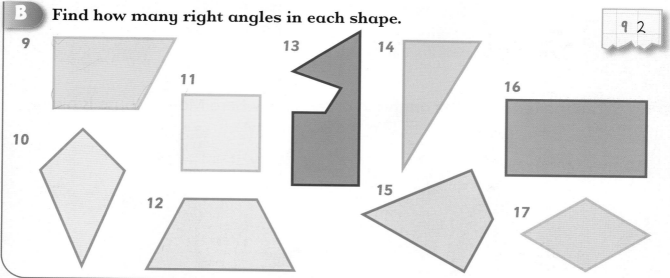

9

10

11

12

13

14

15

16

17

9 2

Challenge

a Draw a quadrilateral with 2 right angles.
b Draw a triangle with I right angle.
c Draw a hexagon with I right angle.
d Draw a quadrilateral with 4 right angles.
e Draw a pentagon with 2 right angles.

Can you compare angles with a right angle, saying whether they are more or less?

A **Write the letter of the smallest angle in each shape.**

1 b

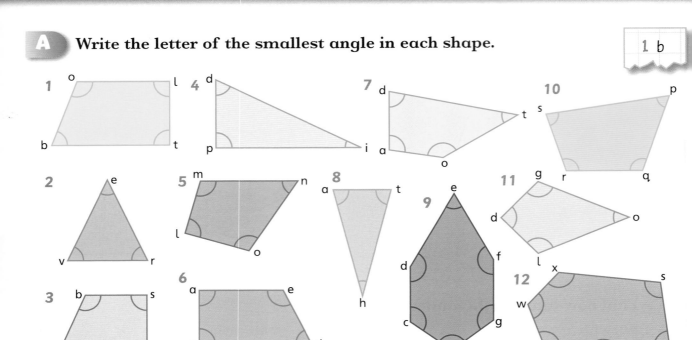

1 o l
b t

4 d
p i

7 d
t
a o

10 p
s
r q

2 e
v r

5 m
n
l
o

8 a t
h

9 e
d f
c g
b

11 g r
d
o
l

3 b s
h t

6 a e
g d

12 x s
w
v u t

13 Write the letters of the angles in order. Find where Molly Mouse is hiding.

Challenge   ⊟ ⊠

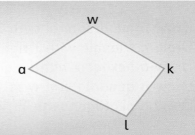

a Make up your own angle code like the one above
by drawing shapes for a partner. Use the letter
of the largest angle in each shape. For example,
w is the largest angle.

b Make a secret message for your partner to answer.

w
a k
l

Can you compare angles with a right angle and identify right angles
in 2D shapes?

A Use the clues to work out the name of each shape.

1 This shape is a quadrilateral with 4 right angles. The red side is longer than the blue side.

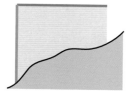

2 This shape is a quadrilateral with 4 right angles. The red side and the blue side are the same length.

3 This shape has 3 sides and 1 right angle.

4 This quadrilateral has 2 pairs of equal sides and 4 right angles.

B Write true or false for each statement.

5 You can draw a triangle with 2 right angles.

6 You can draw a quadrilateral with 3 right angles.

7 You can draw a pentagon with 2 right angles.

8 You can draw a hexagon with 3 right angles.

9 You can draw a pentagon with 3 right angles.

10 You can draw a quadrilateral with 4 equal sides and no right angles.

C Use a paper right angle.

11 Fold the paper in half to make a half right angle.

12 Draw 10 angles that are larger than 45° but smaller than a right angle.

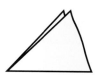

Challenge

a Without moving from your seat, write 20 different angles that you think will be right angles.

b Write 10 right angles you can touch without moving from your seat.

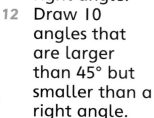

Can you investigate general statements about shapes and suggest examples to match them?

A Write in order, smallest amount first.

1 £650 £506 £156 £605 £666
2 £481 £184 £480 £841 £148
3 £307 £73 £703 £37 £713
4 £556 £665 £565 £656 £555
5 £927 £903 £899 £972 £99

B Answer these.

6 137 + 20
7 155 + 40
8 118 + 70
9 234 + 11
10 625 − 11

11 637 − 9
12 28 + 19
13 70 − 31
14 63 − 21
15 36 + 49

C Answer these. Show your working.

16 127 + 61
17 224 + 38
18 343 + 45
19 68 + 150
20 64 + 164
21 457 + 39

D Find the larger capacity.

22 600 ml or $\frac{1}{2}$ l
23 $\frac{1}{4}$ l or 300 ml
24 480 ml or $\frac{1}{2}$ l
25 1 l or 1050 ml
26 $\frac{3}{4}$ l or 600 ml
27 $\frac{1}{4}$ l or 200 ml

E Copy these half shapes and the line of symmetry on squared paper. Complete each shape.

28 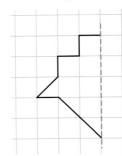   29

F Find which direction the arrow will point after turning:

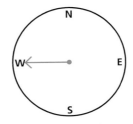

30 2 right angles anti-clockwise
31 3 right angles clockwise.

G Find how many right angles in each shape.

32 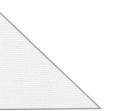   34

33    35

A Answer these.

1 Which numbers in the orange box are multiples of 2?
2 Which numbers in the green box are multiples of 10?
3 Which numbers in the orange box are multiples of 5?
4 Which numbers in the green box are odd numbers?

Orange box:
100 2 7
65 32 40
16
78 46 55
25

Green box:
28 42 80
51
60 35
90
64
120 30
85

B Joe, Ellie and Sanjay are saving coins. Using their coins, find which amounts in the box could be paid exactly by:

5 Ellie   6 Joe   7 Sanjay.

60p 58p 75p 30p 25p 46p 90p 52p 35p £1

C Write 3 different ways that together:

> 8 3 5p and 11 2p coins
> 7 5p and 1 2 coins
> 5 5p and 6 2p coins

8 Ellie and Joe can pay 37p
9 Ellie and Joe can pay 49p
10 Ellie and Sanjay can pay 56p.

D Write the different amounts you can pay exactly if you have:

11 two 10p coins and two 5p coins
12 two 10p coins, two 5p coins and two 2p coins.

Challenge — ×

Play with a partner. Use number cards 0 to 9. Take turns to shuffle the cards and turn over the top 2. If you can arrange your cards to make:
• a multiple of 2, score 2 points
• a multiple of 5, score 5 points
• a multiple of 10, score 10 points.
The first to score 50 points wins the game. For example,

5 2

2 5   multiple of 5 – score 5 points

5 2   multiple of 2 – score 2 points
Total score 7 points

Can you recognize 2-digit multiples of 2, 5 and 10 and solve mathematical problems?

107

A Write the next 3 numbers in each sequence.

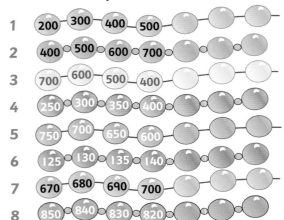

1 200 300 400 500
2 400 500 600 700
3 700 600 500 400
4 250 300 350 400
5 750 700 650 600
6 125 130 135 140
7 670 680 690 700
8 850 840 830 820

B Find the multiple of 10 after:

9 120
10 80
11 40
12 100
13 180
14 360

C Find the multiple of 100 before:

15 700
16 200
17 800
18 400
19 900
20 1000

D Find the multiple of 50 after:

21 600
22 250
23 100
24 750
25 800
26 50

E Answer these.

27 Write four different multiples of 10 between 100 and 150.
28 Write four different multiples of 100 greater than 500.
29 Write four different multiples of 50 less than 350.
30 Write four different multiples of 100 less than 600.

Challenge ⊟⊠

Using only 5p, 10p, 50p and £1 coins, write 5 different ways to pay for each.

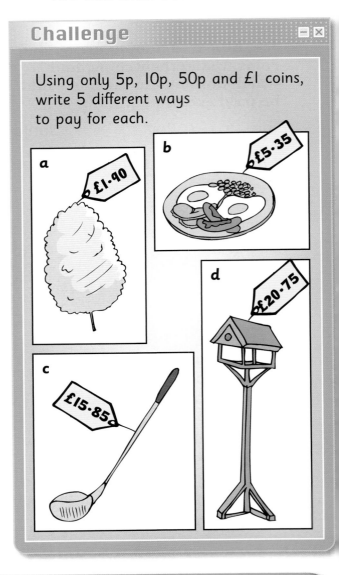

a £1·90

b £5·35

c £15·85

d £20·75

Can you recognize 2- and 3-digit multiples of 2, 5 or 10 and 3-digit multiples of 50 and 100?

A Look at this shape.

1 Find how to put the numbers 1 to 8 in the circles so that the numbers on each side of the square add up to 13.

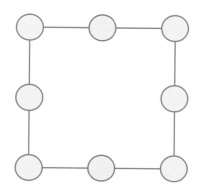

B Copy this magic square.

2 Complete the square so that the 3 numbers in any direction add up to 21.

4		8
	7	
6		

C This lift is for minibeasts only.

3 2 spiders, 1 ant and 2 mice

3 How many different ways can you find to fill the lift?

4 How many different ways can you find to fill the lift if 40 legs are allowed?

LIFT
spiders, mice and ants only
max. 30 legs

D Look at this pentagon.

5 Find how to put the numbers 1 to 10 in the circles so that the numbers on each side of the pentagon add up to 14.

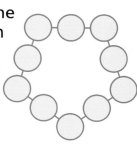

Challenge

☐ ☒

Find the missing digits.

a 1⬤ + ◼4 = 27
b ⬤4 + 2⬤ = 55
c 4⬤ − ◼9 = 15

d ⬤8 − 3⬤ = 46
e ⬤4 − 1⬤ = 37
f 4✿ − ◼6 = 17

g 2▨ + ⬤8 = 51
h ⬤4 + 4⬟ = 81

Can you solve mathematical problems or puzzles, recognize simple patterns and relationships, generalize and predict?

109

A Answer these.

| 1 6 |

1 30 ÷ 5   8 50 ÷ 10
2 28 ÷ 4   9 18 ÷ 2
3 20 ÷ 2   10 45 ÷ 5
4 50 ÷ 5   11 36 ÷ 4
5 21 ÷ 3
6 32 ÷ 4
7 24 ÷ 4

B Write 2 multiplication facts and 2 division facts that link these numbers.

12 **2, 40, 80**
13 **3, 30, 90**
14 **5, 50, 250**
15 **2, 70, 140**
16 **4, 40, 160**
17 **3, 50, 150**
18 **5, 60, 300**

12 40 × 2 = 80
     2 × 40 = 80
     80 ÷ 2 = 40
     80 ÷ 40 = 2

C Answer these.

| 19 80 |

19 20 × 4   23 30 × 2
20 40 × 4   24 40 × 5
21 50 × 3   25 80 ÷ 10   27 100 ÷ 10
22 60 × 5   26 60 ÷ 10   28 40 ÷ 5

D Solve these problems.

29 How many teams are there when 28 children are put into teams of 4?
30 How many each when 5 children have an equal share of 30 toffees?
31 How many each when 4 spiders have an equal share of 80 flies?
32 How many each when 3 farmers have an equal share of 150 sheep?

Challenge   − ×

a Find how many bees will be in each group if all the bees in the hive are divided into:
   • 2 equal groups
   • 3 equal groups
   • 5 equal groups
   • 10 equal groups.
b How many bees will be left over if the bees in the hive are divided into 4 equal groups?

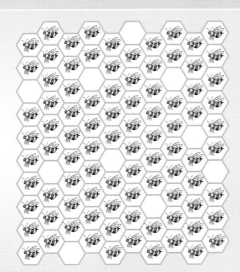

Can you use known number facts and place value to carry out simple multiplications and divisions?

A Work out these divisions.

1 26 ÷ 3
2 18 ÷ 4

| 1 8 remainder 2 |

3 26 ÷ 5
4 33 ÷ 4   7 27 ÷ 2   10 39 ÷ 5
5 58 ÷ 10   8 30 ÷ 4   11 99 ÷ 10
6 44 ÷ 5   9 62 ÷ 10

B Find how many each and how many left over when:

| 12 9 sweets each, 1 left over |

12 46 sweets are shared equally among 5 children
13 105 books are shared equally among 10 classes
14 37 custard pies are shared equally among 4 clowns
15 32 buns are shared equally among 3 elephants.

C Find how many packs and how many left over when:

| 16 8 packs and 6 left over |

16 86 mints are packed in tens
17 48 apples are packed in fives
18 423 pins are packed in hundreds
19 33 cakes are packed in twos
20 31 biros are packed in fours
21 25 bulbs are packed in threes.

D Write a division that leaves a remainder of:

| 22 18 ÷ 4 |

22 2   24 3   26 9
23 1   25 4   27 7

E Write 5 numbers that have a remainder of 1 when they are divided by:

28 **2**   30 **10**   32 **3**

29 **4**   31 **5**

F Find the biggest remainder you can get when you divide by:

33 3   35 5   37 4
34 2   36 10

Challenge ▬ ✕

a Find a number that can be divided by 2, 3, 4, 5 or 10 without leaving a remainder.
b Find a number less than 50 that leaves a remainder of 1 when it is divided by 2, 3 or 4, a remainder of 2 when it is divided by 5 and a remainder of 7 when it is divided by 10.

A Solve these problems.

$i\ 17 \div 3 = 5\ r\ 2$ 5 mugs

1 How many mugs costing £3 each can you buy if you have £17?

2 How many concert tickets costing £5 each can you buy if you have £28?

3 Asha has 33 10p coins. If she changes her coins for 50p coins, how many 10p coins will she have left over?

4 Cakes are packed in boxes of 4. How many cakes will be left over when 39 cakes are packed?

5 Lollies cost 75p. What will be the cost of 10 lollies?

6 Leo saves 50p every week. For how many weeks will he need to save before he can buy a calculator costing £12·20?

7 How many pound coins are left over when 26 £1 coins are shared equally among 3 children?

8 I think of a number, add 8 and divide by 2. My answer is 10. What is my number?

9 Declan has a £5 note. He buys a comic for £1·30 and asks the shopkeeper to give him as many 50p coins as possible in his change. How many 50p coins will the shopkeeper give him?

10 On 3 shelves in a bookcase there are 28 books, 37 books and 22 books. If the books are moved so that there is the same number on each shelf, how many books will be on each shelf?

Challenge

Work out the remainder for each division. Write the letter by the correct remainder to find out what is in the box.

a $16 \div 5$ (1A) (3W) (4I)

b $19 \div 5$ (1T) (3S) (4V)

c $37 \div 2$ (0A) (1E)

d $49 \div 10$ (1L) (4N) (9R)

e $63 \div 10$ (3Y) (7T) (5C)

f $28 \div 5$ (2I) (3A) (4U)

g $22 \div 3$ (1N) (0K) (2R)

h $37 \div 4$ (1G) (2E) (3L)

i $37 \div 5$ (4D) (3P) (2R)

j $59 \div 10$ (8A) (9Y) (1B)

k $32 \div 3$ (0N) (1A) (2G)

l $58 \div 2$ (1T) (0O)

m $64 \div 10$ (2E) (4O) (6M)

n $101 \div 100$ (1S) (1IL) (10C)

o $73 \div 10$ (7O) (3E) (5N)

112

Can you use any of the 4 operations to solve a problem and write a number sentence to show how the problem was solved?

You need: a set of 20 counters

Place a counter on the yellow square on the grid.

Answer question 1. One of the squares next to your counter shows the right answer.

Cover the square with a counter.

Answer question 2. One of the squares next to your counter shows the answer to question 2.

Cover the square with a counter.

Carry on like this.

Find out where the police car is going.

stadium	larger	800	145	36	150	6	hospital
smaller	900	70	155	32	600	larger	smaller
1100	15	90	6	3	5	32	33
8	1500	1	2	3	8	smaller	8
sports club	20	24	32	40	4	20	smaller
cinema	larger	28	3	1	45	55	180
60	90	400	9	2	smaller	larger	town hall
	80	200	900	0	café	33	station

1. What is the multiple of 10 after 70?
2. 50×4
3. $90 \div 10$
4. What is the largest remainder you can get when you divide by 4?
5. 8×4
6. $35 \div 4 = 8$ remainder
7. $63 \div 10 =$ ✹ remainder 3
8. double 45
9. $150 \div 10$
10. What is the multiple of 100 before 1000?
11. 100×8
12. Find the next number in this sequence: 115, 120, 125, 130, 135, 140, ▲
13. What multiple of 4 comes between 35 and 39?
14. 30×5
15. $60 \div 10$
16. Is this angle larger or smaller than a right angle?
17. How many 50p coins would you need to pay a bill of £16·25?
18. $40 \div 5$
19. $200 \div 10$
20. half of 90
21. Is this angle larger or smaller than a right angle?

A Write the missing sign.

  1 ÷

1 24 ✴ 6 = 4   4 7 ⬡ 4 = 11   7 36 ◼ 9 = 4
2 3 ◼ 8 = 24   5 3 ⬤ 9 = 27   8 20 ◖ 5 = 4   10 7 ◼ 5 = 35
3 24 ⬤ 8 = 32   6 32 ★ 4 = 28   9 30 ✴ 5 = 25   11 21 ✴ 7 = 14

B Cover the answer to each question on the grid. Find out who scored the goal.

10	24	900	21	25	5	45
2	33	70	80	32	18	160
15	48	9	320	3	4	7
44	27	55	28	6	11	120
700	60	12	600	50	26	8
35	14	30	200	20	400	36

12 6 × 5
13 7 × 100
14 27 ÷ 3
15 $\frac{1}{10}$ of 80

16 $\frac{1}{4}$ of 40
17 100 × 9
18 5 × 9
19 9 × 4

20 double 35
21 28 ÷ 4
22 5 × 7
23 10 × 12
24 40 × 4
25 $\frac{1}{2}$ of 50
26 $\frac{1}{10}$ of 50
27 140 ÷ 10
28 3 × 9
29 8 × 3
30 10 × 2

31 100 × 4
32 15 ÷ 5
33 10 × 5

34 8 × 4
35 18 ÷ 3

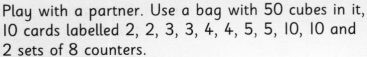

Challenge

Play with a partner. Use a bag with 50 cubes in it, 10 cards labelled 2, 2, 3, 3, 4, 4, 5, 5, 10, 10 and 2 sets of 8 counters.
Take turns. Take more than 10 cubes from the bag. Shuffle the cards. Turn over the top card.
Divide the number of cubes by the card number. Work out the remainder.
If your remainder is on the grid, cover it with a counter.
The winner is the first to place all of their 8 counters on the grid.

0	8	9	1	5
3	1	4	2	2
7	2	3	0	1
3	1	2	4	6

Can you use known facts and place value to multiply and divide mentally?

A Answer these. Check each division using multiplication. Show your working.

1 27 ÷ 3
2 32 ÷ 4
3 45 ÷ 5

4 90 ÷ 10
5 21 ÷ 3
6 30 ÷ 5

7 28 ÷ 4
8 35 ÷ 5
9 18 ÷ 3

10 20 ÷ 2
11 80 ÷ 10

1 9   9 × 3 = 27

B Solve these problems.

18 tomatoes   19 sausages

14 pieces of toast   15 hash browns

23 mushrooms

12 How many people can each have 3 sausages?
13 Each breakfast has four mushrooms. How many breakfasts can be served with mushrooms?
14 One breakfast is served every 5 minutes. How many breakfasts will be served after 47 minutes?
15 If the tomatoes are shared equally among 5 customers, how many tomatoes will each customer get? How many tomatoes will be left over?
16 If each breakfast is served with 2 pieces of toast, how many more pieces of toast will be needed for 15 breakfasts?
17 If 4 people are served with 3 hash browns, how many more hash browns will be needed to serve 3 more breakfasts?

Challenge

Work out which number was put into the machine to produce each coloured answer card.

a

IN   OUT
5 8 20 2 6 10
÷4

b

IN   ×3   OUT
12 3 9 15 6 30
÷2

Can you choose appropriate number operations and calculation methods to solve money or 'real-life' word problems with one or two steps?

115

A Solve these problems.

1 4 children can fit into a car on a fairground ride. How many cars will be needed for 46 children?

2 A stall at the school fair collects 103 £1 coins. If the coins are changed for £10 notes, how many notes will be given? How many £1 coins will be left over?

3 What is the total of three 50p coins and eight 5p coins?

4 Tickets for the circus cost £5. How many tickets can you buy with £63?

5 Rose buys 2 packs of tulip bulbs. There are 24 bulbs in one pack and 15 in the other. If she plants the tulips in rows of 5, how many rows will there be? How many tulips left over?

6 A shopkeeper has 6 packs of 4 apples and 5 packs of 8 apples. If he puts all of his apples into bags of 6, how many bags will there be? How many apples left over?

7 Timmy has five £1 coins. Tony has six 50p coins. Tammy has twelve 5p coins and Tommy has twenty 1p coins. If they put all their money together and share it out equally, how much will each person get?

8 How many sweets, each costing 6p, can you buy for £1?

Challenge ⊟⊠

a If the string around this box is cut into 4 equal pieces, how long would each piece be?

b These 4 boys all weigh the same. How much does Ben weigh?

Can you solve word problems involving money and measures, using one or more steps?

A Make 3 copies of this shape on squared paper.

1 Colour $\frac{2}{5}$ of the first shape.

2 Colour $\frac{1}{2}$ of the second shape.

3 Colour $\frac{4}{5}$ of the third shape.

B Copy and complete.

$4 \quad \frac{1}{5} = \frac{2}{10}$

4 $\frac{1}{5} = \frac{\bullet}{10}$

5 $\frac{2}{5} = \frac{\bullet}{10}$

6 $\frac{1}{2} = \frac{\star}{4}$

7 $\frac{\bullet}{10} = \frac{1}{2}$

8 $\frac{3}{\blacksquare} = \frac{6}{10}$

9 $\frac{4}{5} = \frac{8}{\blacksquare}$

10 $\frac{3}{\bullet} = 1$ whole

C Find the larger fraction.

$11 \quad \frac{4}{5}$

11 $\frac{1}{2}$ or $\frac{4}{5}$

12 $\frac{1}{4}$ or $\frac{3}{5}$

13 $\frac{1}{10}$ or $\frac{1}{3}$

14 $\frac{1}{3}$ or $\frac{1}{4}$

15 $\frac{1}{10}$ or $\frac{1}{5}$

16 $\frac{1}{3}$ or $\frac{1}{5}$

17 $\frac{2}{5}$ or $\frac{7}{10}$

18 $\frac{3}{4}$ or $\frac{3}{5}$

19 $\frac{7}{10}$ or $\frac{3}{5}$

20 $\frac{3}{5}$ or $\frac{1}{2}$

D Write in order of size, smallest first.

$21 \quad \frac{1}{5} \quad \frac{1}{4} \quad \frac{1}{3} \quad \frac{1}{2}$

21 $\frac{1}{2}$ $\frac{1}{4}$ $\frac{1}{5}$ $\frac{1}{3}$

22 $\frac{1}{4}$ $\frac{3}{5}$ $\frac{1}{2}$ $\frac{9}{10}$

23 $\frac{2}{3}$ $\frac{3}{10}$ $\frac{1}{2}$ $\frac{1}{5}$

24 $\frac{3}{4}$ $\frac{9}{10}$ $\frac{2}{5}$ $\frac{3}{10}$

25 $\frac{7}{10}$ $\frac{4}{5}$ $\frac{1}{2}$ $\frac{2}{5}$

26 $\frac{2}{3}$ $\frac{2}{5}$ $\frac{1}{10}$ $\frac{1}{2}$

Challenge

Play with a partner. Use 2 sets of ten cards marked $\frac{1}{10}, \frac{3}{10}, \frac{7}{10}, \frac{9}{10}, \frac{1}{5}, \frac{2}{5}, \frac{3}{5}, \frac{4}{5}, \frac{1}{2}, 1$ whole, and 2 sets of 10 counters. Each take a set of cards and shuffle them. Each turn over your top card.

The player with the larger fraction places a counter on their wall. The first to cover their wall with counters is the winner.

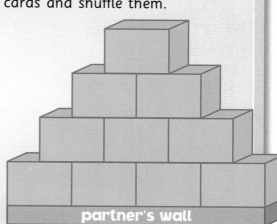

your wall

partner's wall

Can you compare 2 familiar fractions?

A Write the fraction shown by each arrow.

1 blue $\frac{1}{2}$ orange $\frac{3}{4}$

1

```
0 |————————↓————————↓————————| 1
        1/4
```

2

```
0 |——↓——————————————↓————————| 1
              3/5
```

3

```
0 |————↓———————————↓——————————| 1
            1/2
```

4

```
0 |——————↓————1————————↓——————| 2
```

5

```
0 |————1————↓————2————3————↓————| 4
```

6

```
0 |——↓——1————————↓————3————↓——4——| 5
```

B Find the number half-way between:

7 $2\frac{1}{2}$

7 2 and 3   9 2 and $2\frac{1}{2}$ 11 $1\frac{4}{5}$ and $2\frac{1}{5}$.

8 4 and 5   10 $3\frac{1}{5}$ and $3\frac{3}{5}$

Challenge

a At each planet, follow the larger fraction. What happens to the rocket?

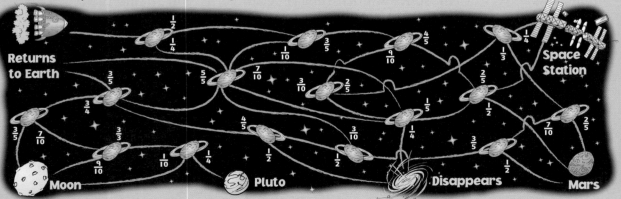

b What happens to the rocket if you follow the smaller fraction at each planet?

Can you compare familiar fractions and do you know where a number lies on a number line?

A **Find what fraction of each cake has been eaten.**

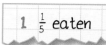

1 $\frac{1}{5}$ eaten

1 $\frac{4}{5}$ left

2 $\frac{2}{3}$ left

3 $\frac{1}{4}$ left

4 $\frac{3}{10}$ left

5 $\frac{2}{5}$ left

B **Guess what fraction of each cake has been eaten.**

6

7

8

9

C **Guess the fraction of each flag that is yellow.**

10
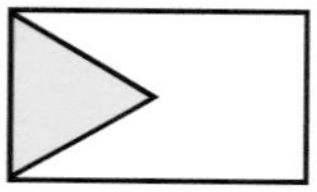

11
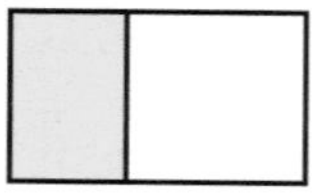

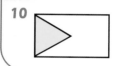

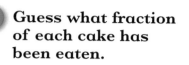

12
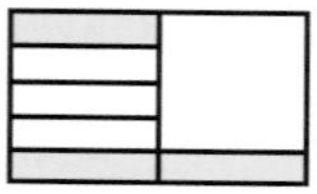

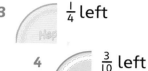

13

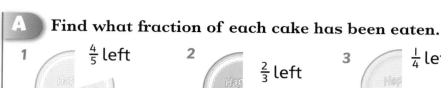

14
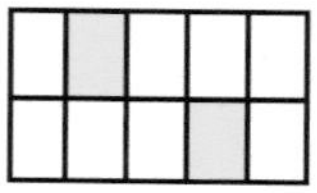

15
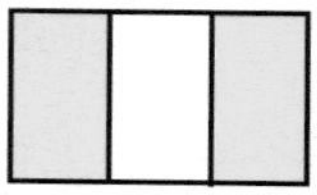

D **A jar holds 50 marbles. Guess the number of marbles in each jar.**

16

17

18

19

20

E **Guess the fraction of the group that are:**

21 red ants

22 blue fish

23 green counters.
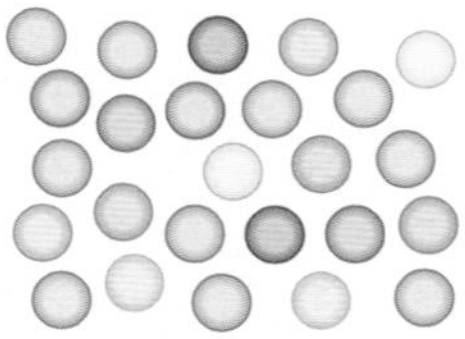

24 Work out if each guess was correct, too high or too low.

Challenge

Explain how:

a 4 children can have an equal share of 10 cakes

b 5 children can have an equal share of 7 pizzas

c 3 children can have an equal share of 5 cakes.

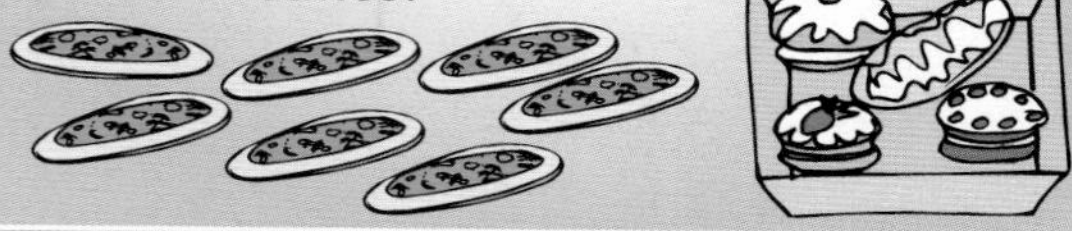

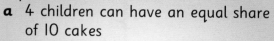

A fraction of a shape

You need:
- a partner
- a set of 16 cards labelled: 1 whole, $\frac{1}{2}$, $\frac{1}{2}$, $\frac{1}{3}$, $\frac{2}{3}$, $\frac{1}{4}$, $\frac{3}{4}$, $\frac{1}{5}$, $\frac{2}{5}$, $\frac{3}{5}$, $\frac{4}{5}$, $\frac{1}{10}$, $\frac{3}{10}$, $\frac{7}{10}$, $\frac{9}{10}$, $\frac{10}{10}$
- 2 sets of 12 counters

Shuffle the cards and spread them out face down.

Take turns. Turn over one card.

Find the shape on the grid that has this fraction coloured.

Cover it with a counter.

The first to form an unbroken straight line of 3 counters is the winner.

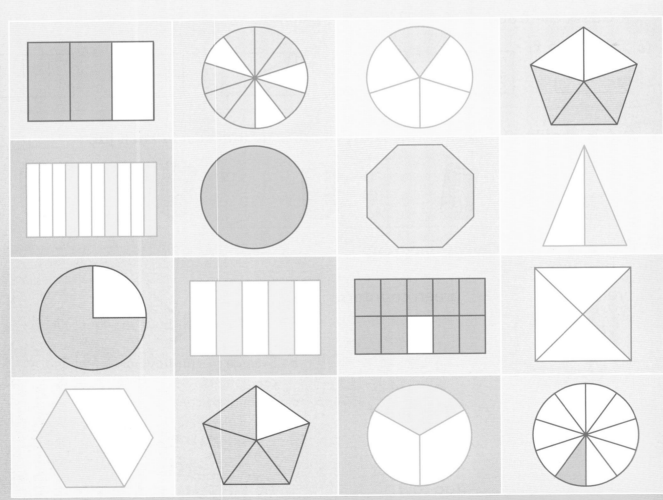

A Find the missing number.

1. $116 + 50 = $ 🔴
2. $210 + $ ⬡ $ = 300$
3. $150 + $ ▲ $ = 320$
4. $400 + 36 = $ ◇
5. $800 + 39 = $ ◼

6. $600 + 300 = $ 🌙
7. $500 + 700 = $ ✳
8. $700 - $ ⭐ $ = 200$
9. ◻ $ - 400 = 300$
10. 🔵 $ - 300 = 800$

B Work out each answer. Which balloon does each arrow burst?

11 purple

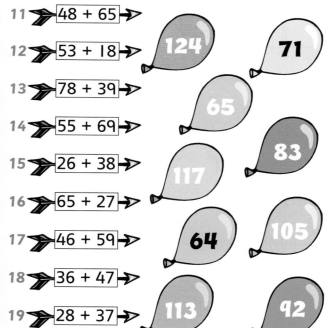

11. 48 + 65
12. 53 + 18
13. 78 + 39
14. 55 + 69
15. 26 + 38
16. 65 + 27
17. 46 + 59
18. 36 + 47
19. 28 + 37

Balloons: 124, 71, 65, 83, 117, 64, 105, 113, 92

C Find the missing number.

20. $245 + 20 = $ ▲
21. $327 - 8 = $ ✳
22. $61 - 9 = $ ✳
23. $79 - 70 = $ ◼

24. $40 + $ 🔴 $ = 99$
25. 🔵 $ + 32 = 92$
26. $502 - 497 = $ 🔴
27. $606 - 594 = $ 🌙

D Answer these. Show your working.

28. $87 - 43$
29. $58 - 25$
30. $71 - 32$
31. $94 - 66$
32. $65 - 29$
33. $81 - 37$
34. $65 - 17$
35. $82 - 37$
36. $95 - 28$

E Use addition to check your answer to:

37. question 28
38. question 30
39. question 32
40. question 33
41. question 34
42. question 36.

Challenge ▭ ☒

Answer each question in brackets. Use this code-breaking machine to work out what the cat is saying to the mouse.

$(45 + 37)$ $(126 + 34)$ $(132 + 39)$
$(39 + 43)$ $(38 + 264)$ $(57 + 136)$
$(56 + 104)$ $(57 + 114)$ $(326 + 295)$
$(98 + 62)$ $(86 + 378)$
$(246 + 179)$ $(337 + 248)$ $(349 + 272)$
$(59 + 58)$ $(427 + 385)$ $(606 + 194)$
$(267 + 318)$ $(45 + 115)$ $(363 + 449)$

a 621	b 860	c 800	d 821	e 812
f 181	g 60	h 171	i 82	j 385
k 193	l 364	m 564	n 302	o 425
p 106	q 721	r 117	s 72	t 160
u 585	v 260	w 92	x 685	y 464

Can you use known number facts and place value to add/subtract mentally? Can you use informal pencil and paper methods to support and record TU–TU?

121

A Answer these. Show your working.

1 347 – 35

2 575 – 43

3 482 – 37

4 616 – 39

5 327 – 54

6 506 – 72

7 453 – 78

8 726 – 59

9 804 – 98

10 432 – 34

11 632 – 77

12 980 – 97

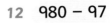

Challenge

Use number cards 1 to 9 and a large copy of this grid.
Shuffle the cards. Place the top 5 cards on the grid.
Work out the difference between your 2 numbers.
Your partner now takes a turn.
The player with the greater difference scores a point.
The first player to score 7 points wins the game.

1st number			2nd number	
1st card	2nd card	3rd card	4th card	5th card

Can you use informal paper and pencil methods to support, record or explain HTU–TU?

A Find how many days in:

1 January
2 April
3 June
4 August

5 October
6 December
7 one year
8 a leap year.

1 31

B Give the month before:

9 April
10 June
11 December
12 March.

C

This is the calendar for the first 3 months of the year 3000.

January

S	2	9	16	23	30
M	3	10	17	24	31
T	4	11	18	25	
W	5	12	19	26	
T	6	13	20	27	
F	7	14	21	28	
S	1	8	15	22	29

February

S		6	13	20	27
M		7	14	21	28
T	1	8	15	22	29
W	2	9	16	23	
T	3	10	17	24	
F	4	11	18	25	
S	5	12	19	26	

March

S		5	12	19	26
M		6	13	20	27
T		7	14	21	28
W	1	8	15	22	29
T	2	9	16	23	30
F	3	10	17	24	31
S	4	11	18	25	

13 Friday

In 3000 find which day is:

13 January 14th
14 February 2nd
15 March 8th
16 February 29th.

Find what date is:

17 the second Thursday in March
18 the fourth Saturday in January
19 the third Sunday in February.

D Solve these problems.

20 Michael leaves school at 3:30 p.m. He arrives home at 4:15 p.m. How long does it take him to walk home?

21 A concert starts at 7:30 p.m. and finishes at 10:20 p.m. How long does the concert last?

E Use a calendar for this year.

22 Write down ten dates that are important to you.

23 Work out on which day of the week each date falls.

24 Work out on which day of the week three of your dates fall in the year 3000.

Challenge

a Floss spends 5 minutes cleaning her teeth every day. Work out how long she will spend cleaning her teeth in:
• January • April • a week.

b Terry watches television for about 3 hours every day. Work out roughly how many hours he will watch television in:
• December • a week • a leap year.

Can you use a calendar and choose appropriate number operations and calculation methods to solve time word problems?

A Answer these.

1 Copy and complete this table for children in your class.

Number of different letters in last name							
Number of different letters	2	3	4	5	6	7	8
Number of children							

2 What is the most common number of different letters?

3 How many names have less than 5 different letters?

4 How many names have more than 6 different letters?

B Use the Carroll diagram to answer these questions.

5 How many of the birds use the feeder?

6 How many of the birds do not use the feeder?

7 Name 2 more birds that might use the feeder.

8 Name 2 more birds that would not use the feeder.

Birds that use the feeder	Birds that do not use the feeder
blue tit greenfinch sparrow siskin woodpecker	swan moorhen goose pigeon cormorant

C Look at the picture.

9 Copy and complete this Carroll diagram for the team shirt numbers.

Team shirt numbers

Odd numbers	Not odd numbers
1	

7 15 12 6
10 1 4
17 22 18 5

Challenge   – ×

a Copy this Carroll diagram.

Quadrilaterals	Not quadrilaterals
trapezium	hexagon

b Write the names of as many different shapes as you can in each section of the diagram.

Can you solve a problem by organizing and interpreting data in Carroll Diagrams (one criterion)?

A   Write in which section of the Venn diagram each shape must go.   1 pink

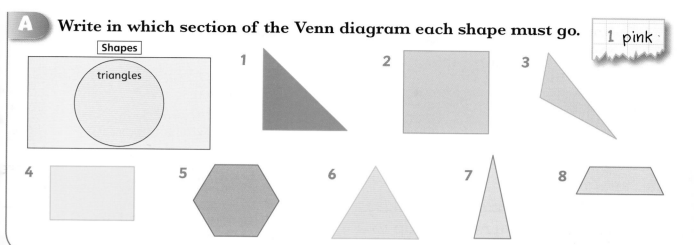

Shapes

triangles

1   2   3

4   5   6   7   8

B   Look at the shapes above.

9   Find how many of the shapes are not triangles.

10   Write the numbers of the shapes that go in the blue section of this Venn diagram.

11   Find out how many of the shapes are not quadrilaterals.

Shapes

quadrilaterals

Challenge   ⊟ ⊠

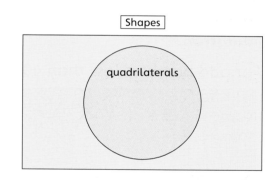

Numbers less than 100

even numbers

Use number cards 0 to 9 and a large copy of this grid.
Shuffle the cards. Place the top 2 cards on the grid.
Work out where your number should go on the Venn diagram.
If it goes in the blue section score 3 points.
If it goes in the green section score 1 point.
How many points can you score in 10 turns?
Can you beat your record?

Your number

1st card   2nd card

Can you solve a problem by organizing and interpreting data in Venn diagrams (one criterion)?

125

A Copy and complete this Venn diagram.

1 For numbers 1 to 20.

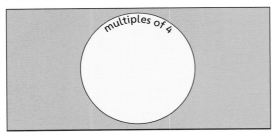

2 Find how many numbers up to 20 are multiples of 4.

B Copy and complete this Venn diagram.

3 For odd numbers less than 40.

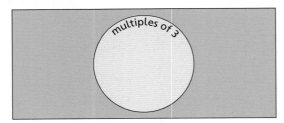

4 Find how many odd numbers less than 40 are not multiples of 3.

C Copy and complete this Venn diagram.

5 For multiples of 5 that are less than 100.

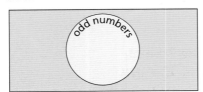

6 How many odd numbers less than 100 are multiples of 5?

D Copy and complete this Venn diagram.

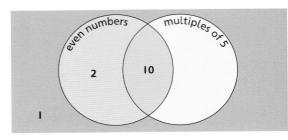

7 Write the numbers 1 to 20 in the correct sections of the Venn diagram.

8 In the Venn diagram, find how many even numbers up to 20 are multiples of 5.

Challenge ▭ ☒

a Copy and complete these Venn diagrams for children in your class.

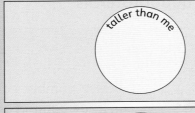

b Find how many children in your class are taller than you.

c Find how many children in your class have blue eyes.

Can you solve a problem by organizing and interpreting data in Venn diagrams and Carroll diagrams?

Review 6

A   Find the multiple of 10 before:

1 **60**   3 **20**   5 **140**

2 **90**   4 **100**   6 **350** .

B   Find the multiple of 100 after:

7 **300**   9 **200**   11 **1000**

8 **800**   10 **900**   12 **100** .

C   Answer these.

13 30×4 15 40×3 17 $40 \div 5$

14 60×5 16 $90 \div 10$ 18 $100 \div 10$

D   Find how many each and how many left over when:

19   35 pencils are shared equally among 4 children

20   33 fish are shared equally among 5 seals

21   29 balloons are shared equally among 5 clowns.

E   Solve these problems.

22   Taxis can carry 5 people. How many taxis will be needed to carry 38 people?

23   Train tickets cost £4. How many tickets can you buy if you have £45?

F   Write in order of size, smallest first.

24   $\frac{1}{2}$ $\frac{1}{5}$ $\frac{1}{3}$ $\frac{1}{4}$ 26 $\frac{7}{10}$ $\frac{4}{5}$ $\frac{1}{2}$ $\frac{3}{5}$

25   $\frac{2}{5}$ $\frac{3}{4}$ $\frac{1}{2}$ $\frac{1}{10}$ 27 $\frac{2}{5}$ $\frac{1}{4}$ $\frac{1}{10}$ $\frac{9}{10}$

G   Find the missing numbers.

28   $255 + 20 = $ ▪   31 $30 + $ ★ $ = 87$

29   $325 - 9 = $ ●   32 $603 - 595 = $ ✳

30   $82 - 80 = $ ●   33 $92 - 33 = $ ●

H   Answer these. Show your working.

34   $67 - 25$ 37 $324 - 13$

35   $45 - 18$ 38 $632 - 28$

36   $74 - 28$ 39 $431 - 178$

I   Look at the calendar.

40   Find how many Wednesdays in December.

41   Name the last day of the month.

42   Name Christmas Day.

43   Name the last day in November.

December						
M	T	W	T	F	S	S
		1	2	3	4	5
6	7	8	9	10	11	12
13	14	15	16	17	18	19
20	21	22	23	24	25	26
27	28	29	30	31		

J   Answer these.

44   Copy and complete this Venn diagram.

45   Find how many numbers less than 30 are multiples of 5.

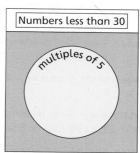

Numbers less than 30

multiples of 5

Glossary

a.m. – short for 'ante meridiem' meaning 'before noon', used to show times between 12 midnight and 12 noon

analogue clock – a clock that has hands to show the passing of time

angle – an amount of turn, flat shapes have angles at the corners

anti-clockwise – turns in the opposite direction to the hands on a clock

approximate answer – a rough answer or estimate near to the exact answer

array – a regular arrangement of objects in rows and columns

axis (axes) – graphs have two axes, one horizontal and one vertical

bar chart – a graph that uses bars or columns to show information

capacity – the amount a container holds, measured in l and ml

Carroll diagram – used for sorting things into groups, e.g. red and not red, cubes and not cubes

century – a set of one hundred, e.g. 100 years

clockwise – turns in the same direction as hands on a clock

column – a vertical line of objects or numbers one above the other

compass points – a compass is used to find directions; north (N), south (S), east (E) and west (W) are the four main points on a compass

data – information about something in words, numbers or pictures

diagonal – a straight line that joins two corners of a shape

digit – each figure in a number is called a digit, e.g. 26 is called a 2-digit number

digital clock – a clock that has only numbers to show the time

edge – the edge is where two faces of a solid shape meet, e.g. a cube has 12 straight edges

equivalent fractions – fractions with the same value, e.g. $\frac{2}{4} = \frac{1}{2}$

estimate – using information you have to guess an answer without measuring or doing a difficult calculation

even number – any whole number that can be divided exactly by 2, e.g. 2, 4, 6, 8, 10, …

face – a side of a solid shape, e.g. a cube has 6 square faces

frequency – how often something happens

horizontal – a level or flat line parallel to the horizon or ground, a line parallel to the bottom edge when represented on paper

inverse – the opposite, addition and subtraction are inverse operations

line symmetry – a shape has line symmetry if it can be folded so one half covers the other exactly

mass – the amount of matter in an object, measured in g or kg (sometimes people use weight to mean mass)

mid-point – halfway between two points

multiple – a number that is exactly divisible by another, e.g. numbers in the times table, 5, 10, 15, 20, 25, 30 are all multiples of 5

odd number – any whole number that cannot be divided exactly by 2, e.g. 1, 3, 5, 7, 9, 11, …

p.m. – short for 'post meridiem' meaning 'after noon', used to show times between 12 noon and 12 midnight

partition – to break numbers down into, e.g. units, tens and hundreds

pictogram – a graph that uses pictures to show information

predict – to say what you think will happen

product – the answer when two or more numbers are multiplied together, e.g. the product of 4 and 8 is 32

quadrilateral – a polygon with four sides

reflection – the mirror image of a shape

remainder – the number left over after sharing, e.g. $7 \div 3 = 2 \text{ r } 1$

right angle – a quarter turn measured as an angle of $90°$

row – a horizontal line of objects or numbers side by side

round up/down – writing a number as an approximate, e.g. 64 rounded to the nearest ten is 60

sequence – a set of numbers written in an order following a rule, e.g. 1, 4, 7, 10 is a sequence adding 3 each time

Venn diagram – used for sorting things into sets

vertical – a line that points straight up at right angles to a horizontal line, a line parallel to the sides when represented on paper

vertex (vertices) – the corner of a shape, where sides or straight edges meet